The Painter In French Fiction

A Critical Essay

by

Theodore Robert Bowie

THE PAINTER IN FRENCH FICTION

Painters have populated the pages of French fiction for over a century and a quarter. Their literary life follows closely their growth as a significant element in French life. As the decades follow one another after 1830, each new period presents a type of painter who embodies and projects the myths and conventions through which Society sees him at the time. First we have the Romantic artist, with his yearning for absolute perfection, who is followed by the Art-for-Art's Sakist and the Bohemian or Anti-Bourgeois, who culminates in the Rebel of the Realist epoch. Then there is the Impressionist, succeeded by the Symbolist of the end of the century, until we finally reach the Abstractionist and the Eclecticist of modern times. In this gallery of successive portraits how shall we separate reality from imagination, myth from actuality? Transposing the question to a broader plane, might it not be asked whether French fiction offers a valid guide to the understanding of the painter's psychology? What objective value is possessed by these portrayals, which appear either as conventional representations or as poetic and idealized interpretations? How did these conventions grow and evolve, and what relation is there between the literary view of the painter today with that of the last century?

In an attempt to answer these questions (as well as many other unstated ones), the present essay posits several contexts in order to assure a variety of approaches. The painter is first viewed in the light of his treatment as a human and social being. Then the various ways of representing him as a performing artist are examined. He is finally studied as an ever-changing symbolic concept. No claim of exhaustiveness is made for this study, which is not conceived as a thesis but merely as an essay accompanied by some critical apparatus. The subject is too vast to be encompassed by the capacities of an individual student. It has been strangely neglected, however, and this little *étude d'ensemble* has been undertaken in the hope that others might pursue it further.

One whole side of the question, pertaining to the esthetic prin-

---

NOTE: In order to avoid constant repetition of titles in the course of this study, painters have been referred to usually by name only. A repertory of painters, fictional and real, together with an indication of the works in which they appear, will be found in the Appendix.

ciples on which all this literature is based, has been deliberately omitted because the author intends to attack it from another angle. A study of the literary man as art critic has long been needed. Since the position is taken that novels and stories about painters (at least in France) are fundamentally a branch of art criticism, the proper place to assay their validity in general terms and, incidentally, to form judgments about the artistic competence of their authors, would be another *étude d'ensemble*, now under preparation, on the subject of "The Painter and the Literary Art Critic in France."

* * * * *

There is a certain unity in the French fiction about the painter which is not immediately apparent because of the variations inherent in its classification. The painter occurs either 1) as protagonist in a work completely devoted to him and his type (*Manette Salomon*[1] is the standard work in this class) ; or 2) as a principal or secondary character in a work in which the emphasis is on him as a human being rather than as an artist (*Fort Comme la Mort* is an example of this type) ; or 3) he may appear as a representative figure in a work which purports to describe French society at a given epoch (as in *La Comédie Humaine*[2] or *Les Hommes de Bonne Volonté*).

The unity of the treatment consists first in the realistic and analytic approach to the subject. There exists for the painter no broad synthesis of the kind made of the musician by Romain Rolland in *Jean-Christophe.* The "historical" method is also little used, in the sense that the model is rarely chosen from among painters of the past, but most frequently from figures contemporaneous with the author. The latter is therefore a reporter who describes artists as he knows them. His method of direct observation implies first-hand documentation at the source, which in turn implies a certain amount of collaboration, witting or unwitting, on the part of the painter. The tendency of authors other than French, in choosing historical models, is to rely heavily on written documentation—Journals, Memoirs, Correspondence, Archives—and often to paraphrase this particular kind of first-hand material. The result tends to be a novelized biography, blending facts with imaginative interpretations. This kind of book is not unknown in French literature, but as far as the painter is concerned, there are no distinguished examples; about the only one that can be mentioned is Fabre's *Le Roman d'un Peintre*, of which neither the subject nor the treatment is memorable.

The fiction is historical only in the sense that it reflects, with a slight time lag, developments observable in the field of art. Thus in *La Comédie Humaine* we get a general idea of the Parisian art world between 1810 and 1840. *Manette Salomon* is important for the specialized history of French painting between 1840 and 1860 which it gives. The story of Impressionism and Post-Impressionism, in the works of Burty, Duranty and Proust, confirms and completes the standard accounts. In short, our view of modern French painting may be considerably illumined by the direct or oblique light provided by this literature.

Unity is further enhanced by two other factors. French literature being self-conscious and cumulative, it is interesting but not surprising to perceive the debt owed to Balzac and more particularly to the Goncourts by many novelists who choose the subject of the painter. To use an appropriate simile, it might be said that Balzac sketched in the broad outlines of the subject and that the Goncourts fixed its tonal harmonies. The truth of this observation will be apparent in the course of this study. The other factor making for homogeneity is the oneness of purpose of a great part of this fiction. The authors' motivations have usually been to attack, defend or champion certain painters and certain schools of painting. These books therefore have in common not only a polemical quality but also a claim to be regarded as a special branch of art criticism. Most of these authors performed as regular art critics in the periodical press at one moment or another of their literary careers; this correlation of activities is not frequently seen in countries other than France.

Unity of treatment is finally visible in the similarity of the devices used to examine a painter in the fictional mode. There are ten such devices, and while only two works (*Manette Salomon* and *L'Œuvre*) employ every single one of them, all the other works use a majority of them in combination, with differences of emphasis. A formal synthesis of these ingredients follows:

1) a description of the painter's early days and of his training in art school;

2) a description of his *milieu*, which breaks down into:

a) his studio; a monograph on this subtopic would show

how the Romantic conception of the artist's atelier as a joint alchemist's den, private museum and seduction chamber (best rendered by Gautier in his poem *Albertus*[3]), gives way to the Naturalists' functional workshop and eventually loses most of its importance;

b) his points of contact with Nature, either in the form of an open-air studio, or the "motif" he chooses, usually in the Forest of Fontainebleau or, when the idea of Nature is broadened to include cities, the Parisian scene;

c) his points of contact with fellow-craftsmen, usually cafés;

3) the faithful notation of shop-talk with other painters and with models and dealers. Such recordings, likely to be of the greatest interest, are scarcely to be found elsewhere than in fiction and constitute an eminent service rendered to the history of art;

4) lengthy discussions of esthetic and technical questions; these may be presented directly by an artist (more or less under his own guise), or obliquely by an author's mouthpiece. The most famous in the latter group are the harangues or quasi-lectures delivered by Chassagnol in *Manette Salomon*;

5) a tendency, beginning with the Goncourts, towards violent criticism of the entire official system and the academic tradition;

6) lengthy accounts of *Salons* and exhibitions, with a description of the working of the jury system. The specific climate and atmosphere of a given moment in art history (as for instance that of the *Salon des Refusés* of 1863 in *L'Œuvre*) is preserved in careful detail;

7) the introduction of literary figures as foils to the painter;

8) involvement of the artist in sentimental complications, usually of a kind which threatens his artistic integrity;

9) the introduction of actual painters, either under their own names or transparent disguises, both for the sake of the plot and for the purposes of verisimilitude; and, finally, their use as elements of composite portraits in the case of leading characters.

This last device is universally used, to such an extent that one may well ask whether most of this fiction does not belong to the class of the *roman à clef*. Actually, only *La Ville Lumière*, by Camille Mauclair, clearly falls in this category; also, in *Les Hommes de Bonne Volonté,* the author's intention of satirizing Picasso under the name of Ortegal is distinctly discernible. Further exceptions must be made for biographical novels, of which the number is very small. Aside from these cases, authors rarely use a single model for their painters. It has been possible to identify some of the real artists serving as a basis for the fictive ones. We know, for example, that Modrulleau in *Les Montparnos* is mostly Modigliani, but we also know that he has something of Utrillo in his makeup. It is clear that something of Delacroix has gone into the creation of Joseph Bridau in *La Rabouilleuse,* and that half-a-dozen or more painters are inextricably molded into Proust's Elstir. The point is that neither Elstir, nor Bridau, nor Modrulleau is definitely a portrait of a real individual. The mere borrowing of certain traits or the use of anecdotal or biographical material, which are standard practices in the writing of fiction, must not be accorded unusual significance here. While the resemblances to living or dead painters are never fortuitous, it would be a mistake to assume that they are too purposeful. The peculiar value of fiction as parable would be lost if we insisted on taking its creatures as literal portraits. This is not to deny the fact an author like Zola could deliberately base himself on his intimate acquaintance with Cézanne to build up his picture of the artist as failure. The amusing part of this story is that for a long time it was assumed that Manet was the model for Claude Lantier. Zola lost the friendship of both artists for this and other reasons. While all this is of anecdotal interest, it is largely irrelevant except in its bearing on the writer's merits as a psychologist and a judge of painting, which may or may not detract from the validity of the portrayal of a particular painter. Models are points of departure, a fact of which we must not lose sight.

There is a final practice which is followed by many of our authors, and which consists in showing their painters at work on a painting. Two techniques are to be observed. One is to take a finished painting and describe its details in the order which the author assumes to be that of the composition. This type of painting is likely to be actual and in a style close enough to the one assigned to the fictive artist. The other technique shows the author substituting himself for the artist and proceeding with an original creation. An analysis of either procedure is very revelatory of an author's ultimate validity as a creator of painters.

These nine or ten factors, listed above in support of the argument that French fiction about the painter should be considered as a unit, also serve as tests of the writers' qualifications. The writing of this type of literature demands more than the usual psychological acumen; it requires specialized technical knowledge, access to the world of painters, broad sympathy as well as understanding and artistic sensitivity. The presence in such numbers of authors competent to deal with this material is a tribute to the French custom, almost centuries old, of close relationship between writer and painter. In the seventeenth century, especially in the category called "la grande peinture," the artist was officially encouraged to find his subjects in poetry, in the name of *ut pictura poesis.* In the eighteenth century a new bond was formed: thanks to his *Salons,* Diderot inaugurated the tradition whereby the writer became the champion and defender of the painter, as well as his interpreter and mentor. In some ways most of the fictional writing about painters that took place in the nineteenth century is an aspect of this relationship. Considered as a form of art criticism, these stories and novels naturally stress the human and psychological side of art to a degree to which formal criticism cannot attain, and they are much more revelatory of the littérateurs' true feelings on the subject. In sum, this literary *genre* is worthy of attention on several grounds, but since the psychological treatment of the painter by the writer is the most important, this essay is almost wholly devoted to this aspect alone.

* * * * *

In *The Moon and Sixpence,* Maugham tells us that the painter belongs to no class.[4] It seems obvious that talent has little to do with being "well-born." Yet, during the Romantic period and even after (including the epoch of the Goncourt brothers), there was a tendency to couple artistic gifts with aristocratic birth. At least two of Balzac's painters, Sommervieux and Léon de Lora, have inherited a "finer nature," an inborn sensitivity which is visible in their person, their bearing, their social grace, and discernible in the refined quality of their perceptions and hence of their work. In addition to "creole" origins (in France this word usually implies colonial aristocracy), which make of Naz de Coriolis supersensitive to start with, his creators grant him an impressive pedigree going back to the First Crusade. Gaston de Chanly is equally high-born, therefore talented, nor should we forget Laurent de Fauvel, though in his case he is shown as too much of a *grand seigneur* to want to paint for a living. The inevitable inference seems to be that all these creatures of finer clay deteriorate *as artists* whenever they are exposed to unfavorable conditions, whether these be uncomprehending wives or a hostile public.

The aristocratic painter is a blood-brother to figures like René, Rolla, Childe Harold, Rastignac, who project more or less the open or secret social aspirations of their creators. Romantic authors were sometimes wont to make much of their real or fancied lineage; as for the Goncourts, they are always suspect of infatuation with the look and sound of their *particule*. An additional hypothesis may be offered for the prevalence of aristocratic painters in this first epoch. Delacroix haunts the imagination of his contemporaries. His dominant figure exercised an influence unparalleled in the 19th Century, even among French intellectuals who cared little for his painting. His leonine though frail aspect, the romantically mysterious aura occasioned by the gossip about his birth, his own personal worth, his aloofness, brilliance of wit and reputation as a conversationalist, and the challenging character of his art all conspired to make him seem the Painter *par excellence*. Though he was a kind of myth who never actually stalked through the pages of a novel in his own time, he was undoubtedly an unconscious factor in the literary concept of the aristocratic painter, at the very least as far as Balzac was concerned.

His type dies out in the novel relatively early, to be superseded by the bourgeois artist (also a child of Balzac) : Bridou, Schinner, Grassou, all belong to the bourgeois class. They all, however, aspire to reach loftier social levels, following in this the trend of their epoch as well as their creator's inclinations, and as soon as they can achieve artistic success with its concomitant rewards, they cultivate their chances of entering into a state of grace like unto that of Delacroix. This phenomenon is observable among real painters of a later generation: Manet assumed the manner of an aristocratic dandy. Whistler, Helleu, J.-E. Blanche, Degas belong in this tradition, which is reflected in literature by the figure of Elstir. The transformation of the one-time Bohemian "Monsieur Biche" into the elegantly austere gentleman, fully conscious of his dignity as creative artist, is merely the latest proof of a peculiar snobbishness which considers art as the privilege of an elite embracing the artist himself.

With the growth of Realism there is a decline in the number of talents assigned to those of aristocratic birth or leanings. There are extremely few sons of the proletariat or of the peasant class who become painters, at least in fiction. Courajod is probably the only instance of peasant origins. As for Claude Lantier, he might with some accuracy be described as a "proletarian," not only because he is the son of a washerwoman abandoned by her husband, but for his constant rejection of bourgeois idealism. Another painter, Delcombe, as defined as *issu du peuple* and anxious to keep the common touch by painting "for the people."

Aside from these exceptions, most fictive painters originating in bourgeois families fail to show a sense of class-consciousness as we understand the term today. If they scorn the middle-class viewpoint in art, it is mostly because this is a commonplace attitude in the artist's life. Few of them carry rebelliousness to the point of becoming *déclassés,* authentic Bohemians or anarchists. The majority of them want to achieve solid material success; if they fail as painters they fall back into trade or a profession. A small number seek revenge on society by exploiting art: Bargue, for instance, having knocked his head in vain against the total indifference of the public, turns dealer and takes cynical delight in urging the *nouveaux riches* to buy the most improbable daubs.

The process of convincing the bourgeois that painting is a respectable way of making a living is a slow one, but by the end of the century the battle seems to have been won. The painters of 1900 described in *La Ville Lumière* lead a normal middle-class life and their problems are like those of any other segment of a capitalistic society. There are socialistic rumbles in the background, but as yet these seem to concern the artist very remotely.

The painter has become too much of a bourgeois also to believe that his professional quality places him in a class apart in society, a superclass, so to speak. This Romantic notion is barely exploited by Zola when he calls Claude Lantier a Poet. Proust's painter is also proudly convinced of his superior essence. The question will be treated more fully below in the section on symbolic categories, both from the standpoint of the relationship of talent to heredity and inferentially to social status, and that of the ultimate function of the painter as artist.

* * * * *

The fundamental need to earn a living while leading the life of art is faced by the majority of our painters. It is perhaps their most pressing problem. Among Balzac's artists, only Maitre Frenhofer has a private fortune enabling him to indulge his passion for esoteric research. Joseph Bridau, Schinner and Pierre Grassou have to struggle in order to achieve a minimum of financial stability, although success comes to them relatively soon. Léon de Lora and Sommervieux seem to be somewhat luckier in that they have some private means. All of these painters are blessed with powerful and influential friends, particularly in the art world. The economic question is never terribly urgent with them; there are no starving artists in Balzac, at least no permanently starving ones. The only one who faints from hunger is Hippolyte Schinner; he is rescued in ample time by the devotion of his sweetheart. The figure of the desperately poor painter unable to survive belongs in the later Realistic tradition.

The novels of Balzac give a clear picture of the close connection binding artistic questions with the economics of society. By 1830 the art world had become in effect an open market. The royal system of official patronage is continued by the state, but there is such a prodigious proliferation of painters that official preferment is obtained under highly competitive conditions, which also govern the non-official or "free" market. The rich unquestionably buy pictures, but public taste is not yet independent enough to accept standards other than those of the Academy. The official doctrines which it enforces creates a kind of closed-shop situation, in which specific values are perpetuated for the profit of a small group. The art-schools, the press, the dealers are all organized for the same end. Originality and novelty are frowned upon, since they constitute an attack on sacred, authoritative precepts. On the other hand, France is beginning to give birth to a remarkable number of independent talents. These restless and disquieting artists challenge the *status quo,* they carry out in painting a species of revolution which is viewed with alarm by decent folk. Bourgeois capitalistic society has one ready weapon of defense which it does not hesitate to use: *couper les vivres,* starve the upstarts. Implicitly or explicitly, therefore, the story of the painter since the 19th Century is the story, first of all, of how he fed his body, saved his soul, defeated the official system, introduced a new idea of Beauty, and died in the attempt. (Compromising with the enemy may be regarded as a form of moral death.)

The pattern does not have this clear-cut, black-and-white shape until the Goncourts' novel presents the facts in those terms, but even in their greatest fury against the Academy they do not demand that it be abolished but only liberalized. The revolt against official standards engaged in by Coriolis and his group, and which condemns them to be relegated in an economic impasse, is a symptom of their dissatisfaction with the corruption of those standards and the consequent debasement of public taste. They would not refuse absorption by the Academy if there was a chance of their contributing to the correction of its faults. Spiritually the Goncourtian painters are kin to Delacroix, in spite of their creators' dislike of this artist. To his own great distaste, Delacroix found that he was being regarded on all hands as the leader of the Romantic movement in painting. After the death of Géricault none better than he typified certain new ideas (which he insisted were old and even classical ideas) : the stress of color over sculptural form, a preference for the Venetian tradition over Raphael, a predilection for violent, exotic, historical subject-matter suggested by foreign literatures, a desire to interpret nature lyrically. Essentially, Delacroix was not in contradiction with the classic aim of painting, the delectation of the mind. His revolution was primarily stylistic and not truly radical. He earned enough governmental commissions and honors early enough in his career to show that the Government, at least and as distinct from its agency, the Academy, was not afraid of him. He never aspired to the rôle of a rebel, and could not rest until he stormed the last citadel. He was elected to the Institut upon his eighth try. Weaker souls would have given up the struggle, but Delacroix was determined to prove his point. Unfortunately, this election had the ironic fate of occurring too late (1857). Courbet had already shown how success could be gained without reference to the Academy. The host of writers who espoused his cause because it was theirs, helped to make Realism much more of a break with the past than Romanticism had ever been. As represented in literature by Champfleury, Flaubert and Zola, the artist is struggling with the harsh economic punishment which society visits on him for his esthetic non-conformism. *L'Œuvre* is a particularly bitter pamphlet, indicting society for its cruel attitude towards the painter who seeks to preserve his artistic integrity, who merely asks for the freedom of expressing his personal vision. He is denied this elementary right, forced to live in an hostile environment and face starvation or moral degradation as his only alternatives. We need but to glance at the lives of Courbet, Daumier, Corot, Van Gogh, Gauguin and many others to agree that such literary portraits as Lantier, Pierre Durand, Louis Martin, Bongrand, Courajod,

Delcombe and the rest are not implausible. The wonder is that so few, either among the real or the fictional, ever compromised their dignity in the midst of the most discouraging atmosphere any group of high-minded and original painters ever had to breathe.

The Goncourts' Coriolis stands out as an isolated figure, because he can afford to disdain the struggle, having inherited a fortune. Until his mistress applies pressure on him, he can practice the creed of art-for-art's sake in a manner unknown to any real painter, whether he had private means or not. Certainly Delacroix could not ignore minor financial contingencies, and even the banker's son, Cézanne, did not behave in quite the free manner that characterizes Frenhofer, a personage for whom he had the greatest admiration.

Since the painter's economic problems center about the sale of his pictures, the figure of the Dealer assumes significant proportions. In his earliest incarnation, found as usual in Balzac, he has Mephistophelian overtones. Old Elie Magus tempts Pierre Grassou by showing him how easy it is to forge Old Masters and to earn material success thereby. The artist presumably loses his soul in the process. This is the most extreme example of unscrupulousness; the mercantile exploiters range from utter callousness to enlightened protection of the artist's interests. In *L'Education Sentimentale,* Arnoux represents one kind of confidence man painters had to contend with: not fundamentally a dishonest person, but driven to the use of expedients of a shady nature. Zola gives us two more clear-cut figures: one is Père Malgras who, hiding his canniness under a veneer of bonhomie, convinces hapless artists that he cannot really pay them more than the miserable sums he offers. He contents himself with modest profits, however, and he is that rarity, a dealer who actually loves pictures. The other man is Naudet, a slick operator who does not know the meaning of scruples. In *Les Montparnos* we have still other kinds of dealers, like Afthalien, the Rumanian (and probably Jewish) merchant who has a real understanding of modern painting and who rations Modrulleau on materials and drink and keeps him at work in a foul cellar, or like Paul Guillaume (an actual person), depicted as belonging in the noble family of the Vollards and the Durand-Ruels.

Other aspects of the painter's economic tribulations are described in *L'Atelier Chantorel,* where the artist is shown at grips with builders and contractors, and in Duranty's *L'Atelier,* which offers a dispassionate discussion of this entire economic problem. For an idea of how the Temple of Art becomes transmuted into a Stock Exchange building, one may also turn to *Manette Salomon* and *La Ville Lumière.* In the former work, Coriolis, who seems to have disdained the commercialism inherent in his profession, is a helpless witness to a clever bit of agiotage that sends one of his early works up within a fabulous price range, at no profit whatever to himself. In the latter novel, we are given a detailed account of how the picture market is rigged by one Héllénault who is a professional art-critic and who manipulates the situation so cleverly that he earns the nickname of "the Warwick of painting." He manages to gain universal respect while extracting gifts in kind from artists and commissions from dealers.

In Romains' Ortegal we have not only the painter who can literally coin money by the turn of his wrist, but one possessed of a sharp sense of double-entry bookkeeping, for all of his casual airs. Ortegal's product is a commodity which must be carefully nursed; he changes his style so rapidly that the danger is that he will exhaust too fast all the commercial possibilities of one given manner. The situation as described here is probably not exaggerated, now that works of art have acquired a subjective valuation placing them in the category of gold and silver as permanent investments.

* * * * *

The painter's interest in the social order is infrequently translated into political action. From David, whose reversals of loyalties were calculated forms of opportunism, through Courbet's foggy socialism and Degas' nationalism down to Picasso's flirtation with Communism, painters have always shown a modicum of political consciousness, but instances like Delacroix' participation in the 1830 Revolution and Daumier's permanent attacks on the régime are the exception. Literature therefore has little to reflect concerning this phase of the painter's activity. In Balzac, the spirit of partisanship is evinced only by old Servin, who runs a painting-school for young ladies and who hides a Corsican political refugee in a cupboard of his atelier (in *La Vendetta*). Changes of régime apparently have little effect, either for good or for bad, on the problems of the art world. The Revolution of 1848, the Franco-Prussian War, the Commune, are treated as inconvenient interruptions, at least as far as the fictional painter is concerned, and his private troubles loom larger than the social question.

Only in *La Ville Lumière* is there any intimation that reforms are impending as well as necessary, and that it is incumbent on the artist to participate in them. The great "painter of the people," Delcombe, expresses a broad awareness that art is on the point of dying, that the Barbarians are coming closer, and that Socialism is at hand. Referring to various nihilistic movements in the Eighties and Nineties, he believes that anarchic principles had stirred up great hopes: "All those subtle people who were bored and tired of breathing the mortally perfumed atmosphere of Art for Art's Sake had experienced a happy renewal of faith in Revolt for Revolt's Sake. But now that was all over. The slow, methodical, dull conquest of Socialism, devoid of lyrical or formal Beauty, was growing daily, and its monotonous flood would submerge the artists."[6] And Delcombe goes on to wonder whether artists will be able to withstand the cold, impersonal rationalism of such an austere utilitarian doctrine. Of course, art will not die, or it would die only if it remained what artists think it is. His friend Rochès is eventually convinced that the painter's duty is to discover the ideas and symbols of the future, to guess at Beauty on the march. "Art means never to resign oneself to ugliness; it means finding beauty in everything." Hence Delcombe chooses his subjects from the hard facts, full of dignity and melancholy, of proletarian life. In these confused statements we find echoes of Proudhon's ideas on the purpose of the Fine Arts, which in later times were promulgated by the collective state.

This brumous anarcho-socialism is also evident in *Le Château des Brouillards,* but here the painters have only the merest revolutionary velleities. In his retrospective novel, André Billy involves a number of painters in a libertarian plot against Napoleon III, but the connection is tenuous and there is no attempt to associate any school of painting with a set of political opinions.

Even Claude Lantier, with his eminently just causes for complaining of the social order, is not driven to subversive action, and exercises complete restraint in the matter of political utterance. Like most of his fictional brethren, he vents his anger against abstractions, like the Spirit of the Academy or Bourgeois Taste.

* * * * *

The austerity and aloofness displayed by a painter who wishes to concentrate on his work do not prevent him from enjoying friendships with other creative artists, especially when mutual sympathy and a common aspiration are present. Examples of intimate friendships, having almost the character of elective affinities, between painter and painter (Monet and Pissarro), painter and musician (Delacroix and Chopin), and painter and writer (Degas and Mallarmé) are too frequent to need special comment. It is therefore to be expected that fiction will reflect that kind of association or its converse, dislike and enmity between fellow artists. Many of the painters in *La Comédie Humaine* like Sommervieux, Léon de Lora and Schinner are close friends of one another, and share friends in other fields. One of the tenets of Bohemianism is the bond which unites artists, poets and musicians; this bond is ever tightened by the trials and struggles of all kinds which each in turn has to face. All the variations of these relationships are played up in the books under examination (except that between musician and painter); the handling of the two other types merits some attention.

The relationship between two painters tends to assume the air of a protector-protégé combination. In *Manette Salomon*, Bazoche is supported and housed by Coriolis, who indulges him as a kind of court jester until he is led to believe that the former has tried to seduce his mistress. Until that embarrassing moment, the friendship which had started when both were fellow students in Langibout's atelier was proof against time and the widening divergency of their artistic careers. Coriolis is equally loyal to his other friends, and it is only Manette's jealousy that makes him drop them one by one, save for the very few who achieve success.

Claude Lantier has a devoted friend in Bongrand, who is an older man and who even poses a little bit as the Grand Old Man of painting for Lantier's group. The patronizing members of this group is the faintly unscrupulous Fagerolles, who has enough of a sense of decency to force the acceptance of one of Lantier's pictures by the jury of the Annual Salon. Towards the end, when the latter gives unmistakable signs of being an utter failure, he is abandoned by all of his painter-friends except Bongrand. Other literary instances of friendships between painters are found in *La Ville Lumière*, where the hero, Rochès, seems to be on excellent terms with all of his colleagues but particularly so with

Delcombe and Brignon, both of them leaders, and with Morsanne, a weakling; in *La Négresse du Sacré-Coeur,* where Sorgue appears as a compassionate friend to his younger rivals; and in *Les Montparnos,* which celebrates the mutual loyalties of the Left-Bank artists.

Friendships between painters and writers form part of a very ancient tradition that has some paradoxical features. It goes back at least to the 17th Century, when *Ut pictura poesis* was adopted as a cardinal principle of the Art of Painting. Since painters were told to find their subjects in literature, the inevitable result was a subtle but perceptible feeling that literature was somehow superior to painting. Granted that relationships between painters and writers were bound under the circumstances to be close, there was a jockeying for position which becomes particularly striking in a period such as Romanticism when the connection is especially close. So devout a lover of literature as Delacroix, who found his main inspiration in books, does not fail to show the effects of this sense of emulation. His *Journal* is full of resentment against the real or fancied condescension of writers towards painters, and of strong statements of his own utter faith in the superiority of the brush over the pen for the expression of higher truth. He, therefore, is not wholly guiltless of condescension towards writers, particularly among his contemporaries. At the other end of the scale we have an attitude such as that of Degas, whose distrust of literature was rather virulent, especially if it concerned painting.

It is a commonplace of literary history that in the 19th Century France produced a great number of examples of affinities between individual writers and artists, implying spiritual as well as superficial points of resemblance. Such couplings of names as Daumier-Balzac, Champfleury-Courbet, Manet-Fola and Delacroix-Baudelaire, to cite only the most usual ones, have to be analyzed carefully lest the assumption be made that they represent identical kinds of relationships. Actually they represent four different types, three of which are not reflected in our fictional works. The linking of Daumier's name with that of Balzac usually implies a superficial resemblance between the drawings of the former and the novels of the latter; in a sense they illustrate and complement one another, because they deal with the same subject-matter. In no sense was there a direct collaboration, nor is there any evidence to indicate a close companionship between the two men. In the association of Courbet with Champfleury and other Realists, we have a deliberate attempt on the part of writers to set up a painter as the head of a joint movement in art and in letters. While this tighter relationship becomes a relatively tangible phenomenon, it has more validity for the writer than for his opposite number; if it were to be exploited in fiction, the place to look for it would be a novel dealing with the personality of the writer. The same observation may be made with reference to the Delacroix-Baudelaire association, in which we have a youthful poet sitting at the feet of a famous painter in the attitude of a disciple receiving the light from a spiritual guide, and expressing his gratitude in eloquent poems and critical articles.

By elimination we reach the only type of relationship which seems to have been of interest to our writers: that of the painter with the writer who may or may not be his best friend, but who is decidedly his critic. In this situation, the writer tends to place the artist in his debt. As art-critic his function is to explain the painter's intention to the public (and sometimes to himself); he may also champion and defend him actively in other ways. What the painter's reaction to all these services may be is not always clear: we range from Delacroix' gracious acceptance of Gautier's and Baudelaire's aid to Gauguin's vituperative abuse of most critics.[7]

In the fiction which reflects these variations, the writer plays another valuable rôle, which is that of foil to the painter, sometimes to his advantage, at other times to his detriment. When the latter event happens, the author must meet the accusation of having tried to "make literature seem superior to painting." This is precisely the remark made by Degas about *L'Œuvre*. But this habit is by no means frequently observable; the contrary would be truer. The Goncourts, for instance, are very curt with writers in *Manette Salomon*. A young writer who haunts painters in the hope of finding an opportunity to launch himself as art-critic is dismissed as "a debutant looking for names on which to hitch his own cumbersome ideas." This sneer could well have fitted Baudelaire who as it happens launched his literary career in 1845 with an account of the Salon of that year.

Burty portrays himself very modestly in *Grave Imprudence* as an art-critic sympathetic to Impressionism and desirous of helping their cause without any thought of self-exploitation or glorification. This attitude is sharply contrasted with that of

Zola. There are two writers in *L'Œuvre,* Jory and Sandoz, both of them childhood friends of Lantier, in other words projections of Paul Alexis and ola himself. Jory is shown as a poor hack who leads a disreputable private life and generally behaves as a hanger-on in the art world. If Jory is really Paul Alexis the disservice to him is greater than the unfriendly action of making the failure Lantier stand for Cézanne. Leaving aside the personal nature of the question, there is no doubt Jory personifies an occupational hazard which many painters have to face. But it is one with which they can contend far more easily than with the kind of friend represented by Sandoz. This is the intimate friend who is convinced that literature is superior to painting, who is smugly happy to see this opinion proved by the material success he is obtaining as against the painter's obvious lack of success, who will thereupon patronize and protect him, and who will even go so far as to imply that he understands painting better than his friend does. In portraying himself as Sandoz, Zola showed himself as novelist rather than as art-critic. There is no allusion to his own experience as a youthful champion of Manet. Between 1863 and 1885 (the latter date being that of the publication of *L'Œuvre*) his whole mental atitude on the subject of modern painting had changed. He had become convinced that it was on the wrong road, and it is probable that he wrote the novel to illustrate his thesis.[8]

There are two types of art-critic also in *La Ville Lumière*: the first one has already been met as the clever and unscrupulous dictator of the painter's market: Héllénault is thoroughly stigmatized as the artist's false friend. The other critic, treated with such tenderness as to lead one to infer that he represents the author, is De Neuze, who meets Rochès at a party and discovers a great harmony of views with him. The two men agree in condemning the gross materialism of the age. The critic is in a position to render the painter eminent services by praising him intelligently in his articles. The relationship is happy and unclouded.

In *Les Montparnos,* the poet Zborowski acts out under his own name the part he played in discovering and helping Modigliani. He lays no special claim to a knowledge of painting. His is a pure, disinterested devotion having all the more merit since he himself is almost as destitute as his friend.

* * * * *

Almost all of the fictional painters under scrutiny here are to some extent involved with women. Three general modes of behavior on their part are discernible. The first one, rarely depicted, shows the artist as dominant and unaffected in his creative capacities by his feminine relationships. Ortegal, about the only good example fitting this category, is a healthy male quite capable of coping with any female; his current mistress, "a tall, dark, fleshy, clever girl," is a good cook and housekeeper with no metaphysical leanings; she is solely intent on pleasing her lord and master, who keeps her from encroaching on his work. She is the perfect antithesis of Manette Salomon. This situation, so lacking in dramatic possibilities, must be as rare in life as it is in French literature.

The second mode is that of the painter who believes in the Priesthood of Art. He does not take the vows of chastity and continence, he is not necessarily a celibate,[9] but he often is given cause to regret avoiding this state. He nearly always has to face the dilemma: which mistress to choose, Art or Woman? Each is possessive and frantically jealous of the other, and each is capable of destroying the man who cannot make a clean-cut choice. Few of our fictional painters, facing this problem, have the moral courage to avoid a compromise. Among those who reject Woman unequivocally stands Maitre Frenhofer; his example makes a profound impression on the young Poussin, whose mistress, posing for the former, begins to realize that she will be abandoned for Art's sake and who utters bitter but unavailing words of renunciation. Among those who reject Art unequivocally stands Titian's son, in Musset's tale. His love for his mistress is so overwhelming that he can even resist her own vehement pleadings to abandon her instead of painting.

The chief examples of artists who cannot make a choice and are thereby destroyed, are Coriolis and Claude Lantier. The Goncourts' central thesis in *Manette Salomon* is that artists should not marry. To repeat their often-quoted lines: "In any household, it is the wife who dissolves the husband's integrity. In the name of material interests, she is the counsellor who urges every act of self-abasement, of meanness, of cowardice, every little compromise with conscience."[10] To sharpen their point, they pick for Coriolis a mistress who is vicious, uneducated, coarse-grained, and to crown the ignominy, a Jewess. "Manette, as a Jewess and as a woman, judged a man's worth and talent solely by the monetary value of his work. For her money meant everything and proved everything. She labored incessantly to place the temptation of money in Coriolis' path."[11] Starting as his model, then as his mistress, then as the mother of his son and finally as his wife, she encompasses his moral ruin as surely as if that had been her real aim. The author's implications are obvious: if you treat art as a commodity, the artist, who is not a producer in the economic sense, goes to pieces. Manette, however, has logic on her side. Being hard-headed, she wastes no time on romantic jealousy of art. On the contrary, she wants Coriolis to work. There is no question of his sacrificing painting for her sake. The authors, in combining misogyny with anti-semitism and a lofty scorn for mundane considerations, had to postulate a hero with a fundamental weakness of character in order to preserve their status as psychologists.

On the other hand, Christine, in *L'Œuvre,* is a romanticist who thinks in terms of rivalry with the Goddess Art. The book abounds in interminable tirades by Lantier, reproaching himself for betraying his mystic vocation by bringing that hapless woman into his life. She, in turn, avows that she feels the hatred of the Goddess and gives full vent to her own jealousy. Her bitterness rises to paroxysmal heights when their child's death is brought about by their dismal financial condition. Her jealousy has also a definite sexual tone. After a series of disheartening failures, culminating in a complete loss of faith in himself as a painter, Claude yields to his wife and agrees dejectedly to abandon Art. Hysterical with joy, she makes him blaspheme his painting, even to the point of spitting on it. She has won him at last. Pyrrhic victory, for during the night Claude hangs himself in his studio.

Such melodramatic treatments of a convention which is almost purely literary become increasingly rare after *L'Œuvre.* Even Zola showed some self-consciousness about its use when he causes Sandoz to disclaim faith in the principle that creative workers ought not to marry. There would in any case be but few examples of single-blessedness among French painters of the 19th Century: Delacroix, Toulouse-Lautrec and Degas. Of these only the last was a true misogynist. The number of happily married painters is sufficient to lend weight to the third convention, that Woman is the artist's best and most unfailing source of inspiration.

Chronologically speaking, Balzac leads the way in *La Maison du Chat-qui-pelote.* The beauty of Augustine Guillaume so inspires Sommervieux that he composes not one but two masterpieces: an interior in the Dutch style, and a portrait of his beloved. This portrait led to the following remarks ascribed to Girodet, who is visiting the painter's studio:

> "You are in love?" asked Girodet.
>
> Both of them were aware that the finest portraits by Titian, Raphael and Leonardo were due to exalted sentiments which, under different conditions, produce every masterpiece. The young artist merely nodded.
>
> "Aren't you lucky to be able to fall in love here, after returning from Italy? I don't advise you to submit this kind of painting to the Salon," added the great painter. "Such true colors, such a prodigious labor cannot be appreciated yet. The public is not accustomed to such profundity."[12]

Love is thus posited as the indispensable factor in the phenomenon of creation. The variations of this theme are developed throughout the 19th Century and are still further exploited in contemporary works. Starting with Titian's son, for whom the experience of love is so sublime as to transcend Art and who accordingly renounces the latter, we come to the opposite extreme, represented by Gautier's shepherd, for whom the identical experience serves as the revelation of artistic capacities hitherto unknown within himself. Monsieur Marcel, in *Catherine d'Overmeire,* discovers the vacuity of an exclusive attachment to Art, and the meaningfulness which his life and painting acquire thanks to love for a virtuous woman. In *La Chimère* Gaston de Chanly is a painter who wants to express the emotional values of modern life. Meeting a married woman, he realizes upon painting her portrait that he has indeed rendered a faithful image of modern woman. The exaltation which he feels upon fulfilling his chimerical quest for lyric beauty in life is communicated to her, and she agrees to abandon her husband for Chanly's sake. When he is killed in the Franco-Prussian War she commits suicide. The story of their lives is told by another painter, Jean Landry, to a group of "decent bourgeois." None of them disagrees with his conclusion that love is the central motivating force of mankind.

Crescent the landscape-painter, Brissot the Impressionist, Olivier Bertin the Academician, Rochès the Modernist, Louis Martin, Pierre Durand, Modrulleau would all testify to the beneficent and fructifying power of love. There is no better restatement of the artist's faith in Woman as the surest key to the divine apprehension of Beauty than the one uttered by Marcel Proust. Elstir's young visitor, it will be remembered, rather resents the fact that Madame Elstir has interrupted his conversation with the great man, and he wonders what the latter had ever seen in that fat, middle-aged and uninteresting woman to make him act so considerately towards her. It is only later, when the narrator has had a chance to see more of Elstir's work, that he comes to realize her full significance:

"Later on, when I became acquainted with Elstir's mythological paintings, Madame Elstir became beautiful for me also. I understood that to a certain ideal type summed up by certain lines, certain arabesques ceaselessly recurring in his work, to a certain principle he had in fact attributed an almost divine character, since his whole time, the whole intellectual effort of which he was capable, in other words, his whole life, had been devoted to the task of distinguishing and of reproducing those lines as faithfully as he could.[13]

The body of a beloved woman, therefore, requires from an artist such a grave and demanding cult that he gives to it the most intimate part of himself. That body contains the whole essence of his idea of beauty. Hence the real Madame Elstir lives on in her husband's paintings; she is a transcendental, immaterial creature. "The data of life do not count for the artist, they merely give him an opportunity to bare his genius."[14] On this noble note the subject may properly be closed.

* * * * *

In creating their painters, French authors grant them "talent" (called "genius" when present in large amounts). It is clear that both words connote moral as well as technical qualities. In common parlance, the painter's talent is a "gift," an inborn sensitivity to color, line, mass, form, and to their harmonious relationship. French literature assumes further that this gift has variations such as a predisposition to favor line over color, or *vice versa,* and that it, or a variation of it, is discernible at an early age: Rochès, for example, is described as "a born Impressionist," because of the "force of his instinct and his immediate perceptiveness of nature;"[15] all this is apparent long before he even heard of the Impressionist movement. The revelation of the painter's vocation is not always followed by parental encouragement. Joseph Bridau realizes at the age of 13 that he has the painter's gift, but his mother, alarmed by the standard middle-class fears, prevents from fulfilling his destiny for a few years. The habit of doodling, or of scribbling caricatures in one's schoolbooks, is sometimes mistaken as the prolegomena of talent: the false career of Anatole Bazoche was thus launched by error.

In general, the painter is portrayed as having known his vocation at the earliest age, and to have persisted in fulfilling it in spite of all obstacles. This display of persistence is an evidence of the basic moral component of talent. Descriptions of his manual skill and the sharpness of his ocular perceptions and of his capacity for developing both, are usually brief. Fabre's *Le Roman d'un Peintre,* a novelized biography, is one of the few books to devote much space to a painter's apprentice years.

To the basic elements of skill and tenacity there is added integrity of character. These three furnish a solid basis for the making of a good artist. Skill and pertinacity alone give rise to the false artist. "Ananias," to use Walter Pach's word, is he who has no scruples, who sacrifices to false taste, who pleases the mob, who yields to Mammon. Ananias even knows sometimes that though his skill be meager, stubbornness can bring him success. Painters like Pierre Grassou and Garnotelle, Chaine and Fagerolles, or Alquier, belong to his tribe; they have little talent but an enormous capacity for hard work. Brilliant but slothful and weak-willed artists, however, also are members of this group. Fortunately all of them constitute a minority.

Integrity of character includes artistic integrity which, according to the Goncourts, has three parts; they constitute the touchstone of an artist's quality; they are: "memory, sincerity, and a capacity for being moved by Nature."[16] Coriolis, criticizing the work of Decamps, observes that this painter is lacking in those three elements. His definition follows: memory refers to that mental operation which enables the painter to be always right in rendering his time-space relationships; sincerity implies the discarding of all preconceived notions before attacking one's subject. As for the third faculty, it is the ability "to experience an almost religious emotion before the majesty of Nature." Its manifestations are "a respectful delight and a moving silence of the soul." Its rewards, a renewal of the "power of vision, of apprehending the beauties of Nature in all her forms."

This third factor is clearly the most important one, especially to authors whose admiration is reserved for landscape painters. It is also basic in any credo which says that the purpose of Art is to express Life. From Balzac to Proust writers are almost unanimous in stressing this aspect of talent. Frenhofer's cry to Poussin, "The mission of art is not to copy Nature but to express it! You are not a vile copyist, but a Poet!"[17] is echoed in the definition of Elstir's work as a creation made up "of those rare moments in which nature is visible as her true poetic self."[18] This capacity for being moved by Nature, so closely allied to the poetic gift, requires an understanding of the demands of the mood, which is facilitated by the direct contact of the artist with Nature. It is a magic process, favored by the absence of other, grosser men, from this locus. Hence the tendency of authors to move their painters to some retreat in the Forest of Fontainebleau like Barbizon, where communion will be possible. "Nature" is capable, however, of multiple interpretations, and after 1850, it begins to include cities. Paris is considered as eminently rich as a source of emotional experience when taken as a spectacle. This inclusion of cities is incidentally an aspect of "Modernism." Coriolis, going through the stages of Orientalism and Barbizon, having become an expert on the Light of the East and the majesty of the great oaks, now stands before the passing show. He seeks "that trait which marks off and designates for art the face of the thoughts, the passions, the interests, the vices, the diseases, the energies of a capital city."[19] The artist's deviation from pure communion with Nature leads to an entirely different goal, an understanding of the flower of modern civilization, Woman. Claude Lantier is showing as going through almost identical phases (save for the Oriental). His own talent, discovered very early and enhanced by his Mediterranean temperament, give him a great capacity for emotiveness and furious excited work. When he goes into the Forest of Fontainebleau, he acquires that "freshness of vision and joyful delight in expression and execution" which are like a rebirth. Thus for him as well as for the majority of the painters, that is, those who regularly seek a contact with Nature, the process becomes a means rather than an end. The latent humanism of the French is never subdued for very long. Woman, Man, and the works of Man are never far from the center of the artist's preoccupations, and the contact with Nature is treated somewhat as if it were a species of redipping in a fountain of youth.

That such redippings are indispensable is implicit in the demand on the painter that he sustain a mood of creative exaltation. Most of the first-rate men created in the fiction which is spiritually of the 19th Century, that is to say, Frenhofer, Sommervieux, Bridau, Coriolis, Lantier, Brissot, Brignon, Rochès and Modrulleau, are preys to a kind of sacred fury when they set to work. This state has not been reached automatically, nor is it continuous. The power to achieve it and to sustain it is tested in struggles with skepticism, self-doubt and utter pessimism. The painter's favorite myth (the fight of Jacob with the Angel) best translates this mood. Here it is as described by Zola:

> "Oh! that effort to create in the work of art, that effort of blood and tears which made him agonize in the creation of flesh and the attempt to blow life into it! Always battling with reality, and always the loser in this struggle with the Angel. Lantier was shattered by this impossible job of trying to make all of nature hold in one canvas; the perpetual pain which distended his muscles finally exhausted him, so that he could never put forth his genius. He became wretched."[20]

The secondary manifestations of this mood are vehemence of manner and of talk, furious gesturings, angry destruction of unsatisfactory work, sleepless nights, improper feeding habits, and generally violent behavior such as is popularly associated with Romantic Bohemianism. How much of this violence is purely metaphorical is hard to say. It is hard to conceive Delacroix, Courbet, Manet or Renoir as yielding to maniacal posturings. Many Frenchmen do express their emotions in vivid language; southerners like Cézanne and Degas live up to the traditional idea of the "méridional,"[21] and least in their fondness for strong language. We must be careful to preserve the distinction between a state of mind and verbal expression that may or may not be a true symptom of it. In Delacroix' *Journal,* an entry such as the following one seems to lend support to the myth:

> "I do not like reasonable painting. It is clear to me that my unruly mind needs to stir about, make and unmake a hundred different attempts before reaching the goal that anything I do impels me to attain. It is an old deposit, a black ferment that requires satisfying. If I am not as agitated as a serpent in the hands of the Pythoness, I remain cold. I have to admit this and yield to it, and it is a great piece of luck. All the good things done by me have been done this way."[22]

This was written when the painter was twenty-six years old, and might be dismissed as youthful romanticism. Yet, thirty years later, on the day following his fifty-sixth birthday, he expresses himself in very much the same vein:

"I was suddenly seized with an inspiring rage . . . . . I feel sorry for those who work calmly and cold-bloodedly. I think that what they paint cannot help but be cold and calm, and inevitably puts the onlooker in an even worse state of indifference and coolness. There are some who pride themselves on this sang-froid and this absence of emotion. They imagine that they dominate imagination."[23]

Such a consistent attitude on the part of a master lends considerable credence to the belief that literature has not tended to exaggerate the theme of creative exaltation. But even a literal acceptance of Delacroix' words should not lead to the assumption that "work" means the actual application of paint to canvas. It more accurately refers to the preliminary stages of intellectual parturition and to the pauses with which the physical process of painting is interspersed. If we keep this in mind, we will not misread the descriptions of Frenhofer, Sommervieux, Lantier, Maillobert or Modrulleau when they are shown full of verbal frenzy. They are merely in a stage different from that in which we catch Elstir or Brissot, for instance, whose serenity is the indispensable mood required for the exercise of the critical faculty. Exaltation does not blot out judgement. It precedes and supersedes it only at certain times. A good description of this alternation is found in *Grave Imprudence*: Brissot the Impressionist, on the hunt for the kind of fugitive sensations which he wishes to capture in paint, tries and fails, but keeps after his goal tenaciously:

". . . . . Then, one morning after awakening in a state of greater enervation than if he had been pursuing a mistress, he went back to Bercy. There, a prey to extreme exaltation, he set down in spots, on his virginal canvas, the tones that seemed dominant; he connected them by the passage of tonalities suggested to him by the principal objects; he sought . . . . . the characteristic details, without deviating for a moment from the application of his personal will. The next morning, when he stopped before his easel, with the picture visible in the filtered light of the studio, his heart missed a beat . . . . He took a deep breath. He had landed in fresh territory."[24]

The true manner of painting is thus a proper dosage of exaltation with the application of personal will; thus, the poet's phrase, describing artistic creativeness as a variant on "emotion recollected in tranquillity," is not absolutely applicable.

Skill, talent, integrity, the poetic gift, are still not the whole key to the psychology of the painter. There is something else, called "temperament," which has always existed but which is not clearly recognized in French literature until Zola as art-critic first formulated its theory. In the second article of *Mon Salon,* under the heading of *Le Moment Artistique,* he states:

"What I demand of the artist . . . is that he give himself to me body and soul, that he assert firmly a powerful and individual mind, that he be a personality who can take a firm grasp of the Nature which is before him and place it before us just as he sees it . . .

The point is not to be pleasant or unpleasant, but to be one's self, to lay one's heart bare, to express a personality with energy.

In my view, all works of art contain two parts: the real element, which is Nature, and the individual element, which is Man . . . Nature is always fixed, always unchanged, the human element infinitely variable . . . . . . If temperament did not exist, all paintings would be nothing but mere photographs. Thus a work of art is never anything but a combination of Man and Nature. The word "realist" means nothing to me, since I declare that the real is subordinate to temperament.[25]

This point of view, largely deterministic, had in art-criticism results comparable to Sainte-Beuve's ideas on literature: to understand the work you must know the man. Either kind of critic must study the man first, and when every relevant bit of information has been amassed, the significance of his efforts begins to be clear. The work is the utterance or expression of a well-understood personality. Zola transfers this theory into his fictional building up of the character of Lantier and never fails to enlighten us as to the development of his personality, betrayed by the paintings expressing specific experiences. This method is already visible in *Manette Salomon,* but is not used in such clear-cut fashion; nor do the Goncourts have a theory of the artist's temperament. Thus the personality of Coriolis is less evident in the works which he is described as creating (and which are always free from technical or esthetic errors) than Lantier's in his paintings (marred as they might be by the author's comparative amateurishness). When Lantier paints *L'Enfant Mort,* a subject presented to him by the circumstance of his son's death, this fact is of the utmost psychological importance. The tragedy has affected Lantier as an artist as well as a human being; since the two are not separable, any and all experiences are transmutable into art, and there can never be any consideration given to sentimental objections based on sorrow, propriety or modesty. Indeed, for the artist the only way to obtain release from private grief is precisely to translate it by the means at his disposal. It is interesting to see the Naturalist Zola thus harking back to

Romantic practice, best exemplified perhaps in Musset's *Nuits*.[26]

In the 20th Century we find Zola's theory carried to its extreme by Jules Romains and accepted with some modification by Proust. With the logic of his relatively cultivated mind, Ortegal believes that all the expressions of his individuality are equally valid. Painting what he likes to paint, without considering aught but his whims, is a process that becomes as natural as perspiring, and precious if the source of origin be regarded as unique and special. "If genius is within you, always and everywhere, why even your droppings are precious,"[27] is his conclusion. This disposes of any need for formal criteria.

Proust, on the other hand, presenting Elstir as a kind of intellectual who proceeds by the method of *tabula rasa,* states that knowledge of reality, whether obtained through emotional experience or by study, must be stripped off in the presence of that reality. "Before painting, Elstir made himself an ignoramus out of probity, *for what we know does not belong to us*" (italics ours).[28] Such an attitude precludes the notion of temperament in any of the senses mentioned above. In his creative moments Elstir makes no display of excitement; the application of his credo requires detachment of a quasi-scientific kind—Proust even substitutes the word "laboratory" for studio. The implication is clearly that painting is the result of a mental operation, in the sense of Leonardo's dictum, "La pittura è cosa mentale." Since, as was quoted earlier, the data of life do not count for the artist but are merely the occasion for baring his genius, the correct way to understand the sentence that follows immediately ("When you see side by side ten portraits of different people painted by Elstir, you sense very strongly first of all that they are Elstirs") is that this ineradicable signature which a personal style constitutes represents his personality. There is no actual disagreement with Zola here, only greater precision.

Few of our fictive painters are so resolutely represented as possessing impressive intellectual powers. Elstir has an exceptionally cultivated intelligence. Not only is he profoundly erudite in all phases of art history, but he has analytical powers which enable him always to draw correct conclusions from the observation of natural phenomena. To a sensitive and discerning intellect like that of the young Proust, acquaintance with the painter and his work is the source of deep spiritual as well as esthetic pleasure; Elstir's painting provides the most abiding type of spiritual satisfaction. With all this, however, the stress is always laid on the painter's intellect as the key which unlocks spiritual doors.

With the exception of Ortegal, whose case will be considered separately, the following generalizations concerning the painters met with in the pages of French fiction might be advanced; 1) none of the good or truly successful ones is portrayed as lacking in intellectual power; 2) none of the mediocre or poor artists is gifted in this sense; 3) an unsuccessful painter is not necessarily one lacking in intellect; the failure is often due to too much intellect, as distinct from specific talent. In the majority of the cases, however, we can only make inferences concerning a painter's intellect. The failure of most authors to be explicit on the subject may be due to a difference in literary method between this century and the last. Proust and Romains, each within a very brief space, give detailed descriptions of the thought processes of their painters; these analyses are much sharper than the considerably longer, but more diffuse, descriptions of the identical processes in the Goncourts' and Zola's painters. The latter are also more interested in dramatizing given situations and in exploiting their emotional content, whereas the former yield to the modern fashion of psychological analysis for its own sake. Concerning Coriolis, therefore, we gather that he has talent, ambition, skill and a sound general education, and that though he has a weak character he belongs to a superior type and could easily pass for a cultivated man. What the Goncourts think about a painter's need for intellectual power may be learned by indirection from their portrait of Chassagnol: this character is so busy spinning out his concepts that he has given up painting altogether. We conclude that the authors think that the philosopher-painter is a contradiction in terms. In this they oppose Balzac, whose Frenhofer is precisely the prototype of the artist-philosopher "who has profoundly meditated on his art." (That such meditation should lead to disaster is perhaps irrelevant; the inner necessity of Balzac's plot does not negate the fact that Frenhofer is essentially a thinker and a man of learning.)

As for Claude Lantier, he is not fundamentally different from Coriolis; both are shown as possessing more temperament than intellect, and therefore dominated by emotional moods rather than by reason. This is very important when the desire is to dramatize the painter's dilemma. The self-doubts with which Coriolis and in particular Lantier torture themselves (along with

Courajod, Bongrand and many others) would be almost inconceivable in rationalists like Elstir and Ortegal. The author of *L'Œuvre,* nevertheless, might well be accused of contradiction with himself as art-critic. If we look again at his article on Manet, we find him referring to this painter as an "analyst," whose work is the result of deliberate observation, reflection and synthesis. Unless Zola was giving in to his passion for the vocabulary of science and ignoring the chance of a very narrow interpretation of his words, he must have realized that contradiction years later, when he resolved it by inflicting upon poor Lantier a disease called "a paralysis of the will," which makes it impossible for him to let his mind control his temperament. Lantier is thus the precise opposite of Manet.

Jules Romains' Ortegal is a philosopher-artist of very special hue, perhaps the only "natural" philosopher-painter in French literature. This artist with the head of a "Spanish muleteer" is dubbed by his admirers "the most intellectual painter since Leonardo," a bit of praise which he accepts without flinching. It is just another proof of his extraordinary and, to him, slightly incomprehensible, luck. As one of the most advanced members of the *avant-garde,* he has always been prepared for failure; instead, he is phenomenally successful. This pleases him, without altering his skepticism or even his sense of boredom. Not that he lacks the urge to paint. *What* to paint is his great problem. He drifts therefore on the winds of chance: one of his greatest "phases" was brought about thanks to the casual purchase of a distorting mirror at the Flea Market; another, to the aimless wanderings of his brush on the canvas. Ortegal is really too canny to believe all the sophisticated talk about his intellect. His mental processes are more in the nature of musig than of cogitation, for he really has no taste for reflection. His ideas come in flashes, in the most popular acceptance of this term. A good part of his so-called thinking is devoted to the calculation of the risk he is taking, since with the monetary value of his painting as a preeminent consideration, any departure from a given style involves the possibility of financial loss. His success obviously depends on his inventiveness; he must be ever new though always recognizable. Any such feverish symptom as creative exaltation must not be expected of him. The only excitement he knows is based on fear, but since he is enormously skilled and prodigiously self-confident, self-doubt, a very momentary sensation, yields to boldness.

* * * * *

Contrary to expectation, the number of times a painter is shown actually at work on a canvas is small. The only real description of such an activity in technical language, with the stress on the tricks of the craft, is to be found in Duranty's *L'Atelier.* This story shows painters and sculptors in the throes of their inevitable amorous intrigues, but on the whole there is much first-hand information about techniques (in sculpture and in painting) and about the costs of models, paints, canvasses as compared with those of the sculptor's paraphernalia. All of this professional detail occupies much more space than the brief remarks devoted to the broader esthetic points raised by the canvasses being worked on by Marcillon, the painter whose studio is described. He is a relatively minor figure, far less significant than the hero of Duranty's other story in the same collection (Louis Martin), but he belongs to the same general period, roughly speaking, the early days of Impressionism. With the exception of the costs, the information provided in this story is probably valid for the greater part of the nineteenth century; it may even apply to our time as well. This kind of realistic detail, however, is of smaller interest than the description of the mystery of composition.

In Balzac we stumble first of all on this paradox that the mystery of painting is described in terms of *decomposition.* Frenhofer is shown in the act of painting out his work, and all his fine exciting talk refers to something which is no longer there. Elsewhere in his stories Balzac favors the first of three literary manners of handling a painting: description, analysis, poetic interpretation. All three manners depend upon the use of actual paintings, usually identifiable because the subject-matter is accorded a pre-eminent place. Description, usually of a finished painting, is by far the most common device used. Most authors employ it for the sake of conveying the particular intellectual and spiritual qualities they assign to a given artist, rather than any special technical or sensuous effects of which they deem him to be capable. In other words, the literary description of a painting is never an attempt to paint with words. The devices of analysis and poetic interpretation are also dialectical exercises which at most represent the attempt of the author to recreate the state of mind of the painter when he was doing the work, and almost never a substitution of the writer for the painter. Zola is the only serious writer who tried to create an original painting for his character, Lantier. Not only was the effort a dismal failure, but it also earned the author the jeers of painters and critics alike. It is the major flaw in a novel which might well have claimed to be the most searching study of the painter's psychology in all literature. The creation of this "œuvre" or masterpiece to which the whole book points is doomed from the very start. The only trouble is that after causing Lantier to conceive a subject which is clearly out of character ola is forced to postulate some kind of hereditary dementia in order to explain the failure, thereby destroying much of the validity of the artist's portrait he was building up. The conclusion seems to be that in fiction a painting can be realized from the outside only.

Instances of the three major literary devices for realizing such a work follow.

The *Turkish Bath* is the most successful painting Coriolis ever creates. It was the hit of the 1853 Exposition and was immediately bought by the Government for the Luxembourg. In choosing this subject Coriolis follows the lead of Delacroix, Ingres and Chassériau, although it is also possible that the actual painting may be ascribed to Bazille:

> "...... On the damp stone floor of the warm room, right on the sweating granite, he placed a woman, seated to look as if she were issuing from a cloud of steam; an almost bare Negress, her loins wrapped in a lively-colored *foutah*, was throwing upon her a foam of white soap-bubbles. The bather, presented full-face, was gracefully foreshortened and curved along the lines of a disk, appearing to be sitting in the C of a lunar crescent. Her hands were crossed in her hair and her upraised arms formed a handle and a crown. Her bent head dropped softly, with the suggestion of a shadow, on her surging breast. Her torso had the charmingly contradictory contours of this bent attitude . . . ."[28]

Enough is given here to show that the style and language are those of the art critic. Here is a painting seen and experienced by sensitive writers who will tell us that the artist, dissatisfied with the tonal qualities he had given to the woman's flesh, begins this painting over and over again, and that it is not until he has begun to live with the model and made her his mistress that he can really express his vision of modern woman. Only then can the painting give off the sensation of warm luminosity which the artist intended. Throughout the creation of this work, the attitude of the authors has been that of the psychologist, the historian or the enlightened amateur. There seems to be a resolute avoidance of all technical details. We do not even know the prevailing color scheme and the tonalities of this painting since the vocabulary used is general: for better or for worse, the Goncourts fail to use here their *écriture artiste,* a method of painting with words with which they had some success. Their descriptive method, however, has the merit of being a fairly literal and faithful interpretation, free from the faults inherent in the other techniques.

In depicting Ortegal's procedure before his canvas, Romains merely analyzes a state of mind which he ascribes to his character. This personage is shown as lacking in intellectual and artistic integrity, though not in skill. In fact, such painters very often possess extraordinary dexterity with the brush—even Bazoche had it, and the Goncourts speak of his "deplorable facility." Ortegal's similar gift is a kind of memory of the hand and of the eye, become almost infallible thanks to the rigorousness of his early training. This mechanical memory functions as a substitute for whatever mental operation produces composition in a work of art. If we accept the theory that Ortegal represents Picasso, we see him in a late phase of his Cubist period (about 1914). He sits before his canvas, with many "ideas" and thoughts in his head, but no motif for a painting:

"Meanwhile Ortegal has abandoned his piece of charcoal; on his palette there is a mixture which gives a grey that has subtle plum-colored hues and an imperceptible tawny quality. (He is very proud of his inimitable greys.) With one hand, which remains both infallible and bored, he draws with his brush an almost straight line, horizontal, two or three millimeters in thickness, about thirty centimeters long, which happens to coincide with the interest he has just taken in his model's forearm without in the least evoking its form. This line interests him not at all. It is merely a jumping-off place . . . . . ."

The painter indulges in some more day dreaming. Then he feels a sense of release, distinctly pleasurable:

"The brush travels to the right in an upward direction. It begins to trace a letter, then another; then the sign +; then other letters and algebraic symbols, those that Ortegal vaguely perceived here and there and that amused or intrigued him. He knows the meaning of some, like "plus," "multiplied by," "equals." Others he happens to know the name of, like "plus infinity," but the meaning he gives to them is dizzying. Finally, there are others of which the sense as well as the name escape him: "bigger than," "smaller than," "function of," but his eye has very carefully retained their shape and their more or less usual position among the other signs.

So, it all makes a volley of symbols, an algebraic bouquet, which is about to blossom in the upper right hand corner of the canvas. It's like the top of a water-spout, but bent at an oblique angle; the drops, which are a's, b's, c's, x's, plus and minus signs, zeros scatter and drop without any servile respect for gravity. A little further on, like an egg dancing on top of a spurt of water, Ortegal places an object which is first a circle, then a circle penetrated by a cone, or perhaps interlaced with a cone, for in order better to espouse one another the figures cease to have two or three rigorous dimensions. Suddenly the brush shifts to the left side of the canvas, and with three strokes draws an eye, which might be a navel, but which is rather an eye . . . . . ."[29]

Here is an example of the creative method analyzed by a process of deduction. Unfortunately it is based on a misunderstanding of the original model's work and intentions which may have been deliberate, since the underlying tone with which the figure of Ortegal is rendered is clearly ironical. But satire, properly handled, can be exceedingly useful for an understanding of its object. This is not the case here. One senses Romains' frustration before Picasso's art, expressed in cool and disdainfully elaborate mockery.

The only glimpse of Elstir at work shows him finishing a canvas. Not much can be deduced from this. Proust supplies us however with some inferences based on interpretations of his works. Like the poet that he is, Elstir treats nature "metaphorically." Symbols being reversible, he treats the sea in terrene terms and the land with marine signs, thus:

"Whether it was because the houses hid a part of the port, the caulking-dock or perhaps even the sea pushing inland as frequently happened in this Balbec countryside on the other side of the advanced headland on which the town was built, the roofs were overtopped (as they might have been by chimney-stacks and steeples) by masts, which seemed to make of the boats to which they belonged something citified, built on land, an impression fortified by other boats, remaining along the wharf but in such close ranks that the men spoke to one another from one boat to the next in such a way that neither their separation nor the interstices of water could be made out; thus this fishing flotilla seemed to belong to the sea less than, for example, the churches of Criquebec which, far away and surrounded by water because they were seen without a town, in a haze of sunlight and waves, seemed to rise from the waters, blown up in alabaster or in foam, and girded by a vari-colored rainbow, form an unreal and mystical picture."[30]

This passage is generally regarded as an interpretation of Manet's *Port de Bordeaux*. A glimpse at a photograph of this picture shows how far the method of lyrical interpretation can take an author. If we relied on Proust alone we could easily ascribe the work to a kind of first-rate Gustave Moreau whose

Medieval leanings had not been corrected but fortified by association with the Plein-Airists. The absence of color-notations, the insistence on the subject-matter, the interpretation of the sensation in intellectual terms all tend to strengthen the opinion that Elstir has been made into a "literary" painter in the best sense of this term which is normally an epithet. In other words, Elstir is the painter that Proust might have liked to be.

* * * * *

Ever since Géricault exhibited the *Raft of the Medusa* in 1819, French painters who pretended to any originality or independence have run the risk of being called enemies of society. Delacroix, Ingres, Corot, Manet, the Impressionists, Cézanne, Gauguin, the Fauves, Picasso, the Surrealists have all had their turn at trying to defend themselves against stupid accusations, direct and indirect attacks on artistic as well as personal grounds, public hatred or indifference, official intolerance, general lack of understanding and encouragement and ridicule. As orderly a citizen as his non-artistic neighbor, the painter typifies the disturber of the *status quo* much more readily than the writer or the musician, possibly because the prejudices of the eye are much more immediately offended than those of the mind or of the ear. The painter has therefore been pushed into a position in which, with the greatest unwillingness on his part, he is made to look like a rebel and possibly a martyr. To his eternal credit he has refused to capitalize on this situation. His very real struggles against the dead weight of an official dogma and the timidities of middle-class taste are struggles for acceptance. The battle is always won by the painter, very often too late as far as personal profit is concerned. Nor is there benefit in this victory for the next independent artist, who has to win his own victories. This pattern of rejection, struggle and final acquiescence has dramatic values which are not overlooked by literature at times when the artist's conflict with society seems to be a phase of the general conflict of the creative worker with his environment. It is then that the painter's novel becomes a partisan pamphlet and that the figure of the painter assumes the symbolic stature of a rebel. Actually, however, the rebellion is carried on against specific artistic institutions such as the BeauxArts Academy rather than against society as a whole. There are no figures in the

French novel really comparable to those of Charles Maitland in Maugham's *The Moon and Sixpence* or of Gulley Jimson in *The Horse's Mouth,* by Joyce Cary. These two English painters (the latter particularly) are authentic rebels; their behavior is consistently anti-social, and convincing in an Anglo-Saxon milieu. It would be inconceivable in France where the artist's right to exist is more freely taken for granted, even though this right does not always carry with it the right of unrestricted utterance. There is only the appearance of anti-social attitudes in the behavior of the Bohemian, who is the standard figuration of the artistic rebel in French literature.

The word Bohemian used in this context connotes two different sets of ideas, which is another way of saying that the content of the word has changed since it was first used, and may keep on changing. In the first part of the 19th Century, and specifically during the so-called Romantic period, Bohemianism is a function of youth, of the painter as apprentice. It refers to that tradition, still alive in art schools, requiring aspirant artists to be prankish and to submit to or participate in complex practical jokes, to talk, behave and dress in conventionally exaggerated fashion for the purpose of *épater les bourgeois.* The earliest reference to this tradition (in Balzac's *La Rabouilleuse*) shows the shy and sensitive young Joseph Bridau, about to enter art school in 1809 or 1810, almost overwhelmed by the older boys' mischief until he is rescued by the master. Between 1815 and 1830 the number of art students increased enormously; since the Beaux-Arts and the various ateliers were located (as they still are) on the Left Bank near the Latin Quarter, association with the University students was natural and easy. The spirit of prankishness, primarily a mode of behavior at school, was gradually carried over beyond student days, beyond the days of apprenticeship into early manhood, probably because this very increase in numbers meant a corresponding reduction in the number of opportunities and a consequent extension of the time during which young men could act irresponsibly. The manifestations of this kind of Bohemianism are generally amiable ones, if we are to believe the picture of it given by Balzac in describing the behavior of Léon de Lora, Bixiou, Schinner, Sommervieux before they achieve success. Even when they are shown to be starving and unemployed, these artists exhibit no bitterness whenever they feel they must assert themselves. Essentially it is the battle of the young against the old, as is clear from the painters' enthusiastic participation in the Battle of *Hernani.* With the 1830 Revolution, however, the struggle begins to take on a political tinge. Young painters, many of them poor, find that the Social Order, which means the enthronement of the Middle Class, is inimical to them. Bohemianism becomes something more than a pose for youngsters, it is a *défi,* an affirmation of artistic and social beliefs. On the part of serious artists it means espousing the doctrine must serve no utilitarian end. On the part of those who carry adolescence and irresponsibility into middle-age, it also means casualness in the matter of sexual relations and other forms of irregularity. Prankishness is translated into roguishness against specific bourgeois representatives such as the landlord, the bailiff, and even one's parents if they refuse their support. All this is crystallized in literature by Mürger, whose *Scènes de la Vie de Bohème* idealize and sentimentalize the situation. By glossing over its realities and perpetuating the myth of the irresponsible but lovable artist, Mürger rendered the latter both a service and a disservice. He took away his potential sting, but he also thereby made it more difficult for him to be taken seriously.

In attempting to correct this false view Champfleury, carrying the banner of Realism, falls into the Romantic fallacy. His Chien-Caillou is an authentic artist, forced into Bohemian ways through sheer misfortune, who exhibits the pathetic side of a falsely glamorous life. The point is made so heavily that Chien-Caillou seems to be a latter-day Chatterton whom Society allows to starve because it has no place for him.

We next have to deal with the false artist as Bohemian. Anatole Bazoche, in *Manette Salomon,* is a very thorough study of the type; almost as much space is devoted to his portrayal as to the principal character. The Goncourts' premise is that Bohemianism is a function of character. Bazoche is weak, lazy and irrepressibly carefree; his origins are base, and though he has a species of talent, he is almost a painter in spite of himself. He is much too fond of jokes ever to settle down to serious work. Supported for a long time by his friend Coriolis, whose own Bohemianism is gilt-edged, he sinks lower and lower, until he ends up, rather happily, as a keeper in the Jardin des Plantes. He illustrates Chassagnol's theory that painters, with a very few exceptions, are a dull race, with dull tastes, dull senses, dull appetites, that almost all of them are *des natures peuple,* which makes them stingy, unimaginative and no better than the bourgeois class from which they spring and to which they revert at the earliest opportunity.[31]

The personification of "la blague," Bazoche is essentially a gay figure. He is also the last one of his kind to appear in French literature. With the advent of Naturalism, the Bohemian who appears (like Pellerin in *L'Education Sentimentale* or Barque in *L'Atelier Chantorel*) is a cynic and not a gay blade, and the Bohemian life, seemingly a happy one at first, is now resonant with the overtones of despair. In the 20th Century, even in the novels which describe the supposedly carefree life of Montmartre and Montparnasse, the Bohemians begin to take on the shadowy outlines of anarchists.

Up to this point the term Bohemian has been applicable to unsuccessful artists, or to artists before they became successful. The term is also applied to the successful artist whenever he maintains a way of living and of dressing which recalls, *mutatis mutandis,* his salad days. This vestimentary and generally superficial allusion to the unconventionality of one's youth is merely an elegant gesture. Many who were once authentic Bohemians and who have now achieved greatness, drape themselves in the mantle of austerity. The final word on the subject is spoken by Elstir, who admits that he is the former "Monsieur Biche," a perverse and ridiculous hack, and who utters these words:

> "There is no man, no matter how wise he may be, who has not at some time in his youth, said certain things or led the kind of life, the memory of which is unpleasant and which he would like to abolish. But he must not absolutely regret its existence, for he cannot be sure of having become a wise man, to the extent to which this is possible, unless he has passed through all the odious or ridiculous incarnations which precede . . ."[32]

* * * * *

The proportion of painters who appear as failures of one kind or another in French fiction is astonishing. Failure is taken to mean first of all the lack of recognition, success or fame during one's lifetime, under conditions where their occurrence might legitimately be expected. It also refers to a situation in which a flaw of character within the artist makes his material success seem to any rational person like the equivalent of moral failure. In the last sense it means the resignation and acceptance of defeat by an otherwise worthy artist, or else the shameful realization on the part of an unworthy one that defeat was to have been expected. What is striking in French fiction is the number of undeserved failures that are pictured. Does this mean that writers tend to take a pessimistic view of the state of painting in France? Here again, the answer is not a simple one, because of the curious ambivalence exhibited by writers when they function as novelists and the same or other writers when they perform as art-critics. Art criticism (when written by novelists or poets as distinguished from professionals and technicians) inclines towards a highly optimistic and admirative attitude towards the contemporaneous movement in painting: Gautier, Champfleury, Baudelaire, Duranty, Burty, Huysmans, Apollinaire are certainly among the most ardent champions of the painters of their respective epochs. We should even add Zola as he was between 1863 and 1866. Take some of these very same writers in their phase as novelists, and a diametrically contrary mood prevails. Part of it may be due to the fact that the failure has more dramatic possibilities than the success; another part may be due to faithful adherence to literal truth as the Realists and Naturalists understood it: to them most of the great painters seemed to be struggling against hopeless odds. Finally there is the distinct probability that the two major works on the painter's life, *Manette Salomon* and *L'Œuvre,* were composed by men who disliked the painting of their times. A careful reading of the Journal of the Goncourts (who wrote standard art-criticism only briefly at the beginning of their career) adduces proof of their negative and grumbling attitude towards "la peinture biscornue d'aujourd'hui."[33] They love art and artists, but usually the art and artists of yesterday or the day before. Those of today meet with their disapproval, perhaps because they are fundamentally classicists and lovers of formal beauty. Chassagnol's series of unresolved doubts on the state of modern beauty[34] is the key to their whole viewpoint, and there is more than one hint of their opinion that the Impressionists' attention to light was a sign of decadence.

Zola's palinody is well-established but insufficiently realized.[35] Not only did he recant in 1885-1886 his views of twenty years before, but he also proclaimed his disenchantment with the direction taken at the later epoch by the promising (but mistaken) artists of his youth. He clearly intends his hero to be a failure, at least in part because modern painting dooms an artist to this particular fate.

Such pessimistic and critical opinions are confined in the 19th Century to these particular authors, but since their influence was enormous the convention of the painter as failure was accepted by a standard literary figure by writers with opposite views. The word "failure," even after clarification, is still so ambiguous that the best procedure would be to recapitulate the principal painters in chronological order and describe each one's type of failure separately.

Heading all such lists, as usual, is a character created by Balzac: Frenhofer, whose failure is caused by mental derangement brought about by a concentrated search for the absolute. Balzac's other failure is a moral one: Pierre Grassou, whose material success grows in proportion to his artistic dishonesty. Mürger's painter, Marcel, fails because of a fundamental lack of serious purpose, while Chien-Caillou is depicted by Champfleury as utterly defeated by Society. George Sand's "Lui" (Laurent de Fauvel) is a weakling who performs so seldom as an artist that he holds the title only by courtesy. In *Manette Salomon,* all three types of failure are described: Coriolis, a victim both of his own weakness of character and of the disastrous trends of modern painting; Bazoche, the slothful and therefore false artist; Garnotelle, another example of moral decay disguised by material success. Flaubert's Pellerin is a failure because Society conspires to defeat him; this is also the case for Pierre Durand and Bargue in Frantz-Jourdain's novel. In *L'Œuvre,* all the painters are failures of one kind or another, even those who seem truly successful: Lantier, who has to contend with a flaw in his heredity as well as with social maladjustment; Chaine, who is a thoroughgoing mediocrity; Fagerolles, who is a trimmer; Mazel, who is an *arriviste;* the great Bongrand, who finds himself in a state of permanent despair and self-doubt; Courajod, equally great, who has come so far as to deny that he ever was a painter. In Mauclair's book, Brignon goes mad, Morsanne is helpless in the hands of a fiendish woman, and Alquier, under constant pressure for funds, commits suicide after admitting that he is a charlatan. The theme of failure is capped in the 20th Century by the pathetic and tragic turn taken by the life of Modrulleau in *Les Montparnos.*

If we look at the opposite picture, we will see a correspondingly small number of authentic successes. Again Balzac leads with Joseph Bridou, Léon de Lora, Schinner and Sommervieux. Crescent is granted achievement and glory by the Goncourts. Fabre's hero could obviously not have failed. Brissot and Louis Martin were accorded favorable conditions by their respective creators, but Burty enmeshes the former in a disastrous love affair and Duranty kills off his painter in the Franco-Prussian War. Mauclair's Rochès is the only one of many among his contemporaries destined for a truly great success. Elstir is shown in the full enjoyment of his deserved fame, but even he finds his serenity disturbed by the realization that true glory may come to him only after his death. As for Ortegal, the author leaves us in no doubt concerning the spurious quality of his enormous success.

Disregarding the opinion of some painters who are convinced that writers are jealous of them and want to show them in an unfavorable light, we are nevertheless forced to conclude that some kind of *parti-pris,* probably of a very unconscious character, actually exists or has existed among novelists. The number of writers who have the most unqualified belief in the superior spiritual values of painting is very small indeed, and their indubitable leader is Marcel Proust, for whom Art was a true religion.

* * * * *

In studying the concept of the painter as genius, we must note first of all that this category is not truly separable from the previous ones. Geniuses could conceivably be Bohemians (Modrulleau is an unquestionable example) ; the majority of them are also failures. Since there are degrees of failure, there must presumably also be degrees of genius. The concept is therefore not an absolute one, nor is there much evidence of a tendency to stress its symbolic or representative aspects—the absence of this tendency being characteristic of French Realism. Until Proust's time the artist as genius is never a Promethean figure, and this epithet is hardly justified if applied to Elstir in view of the comparatively brief space allotted to him by the author. The genius is therefore taken to mean an artist whose talents are richer than those of his contemporaries, whose vision may be more sublime, but also whose flaws of character, heredity and intellect may be proportionately greater, and whose opportunities for disaster are more numerous.

Maître Frenhofer is clearly a genius. He looks the part, as the Romantics defines its stigmata: pale brow, fiery eyes, an aloof manner. He has the virtues of idealism, disinterestedness, magnanimity, a soaring intellect, an immense pride, courage and probity, and a profound knowledge of his craft. He is immutably centered in his search for perfection, holding to the highest criteria imaginable. Nothing can distract him. He is the High Priest of Art, who can have no mistress, friend or disciple, and whose ascetic loneliness makes him comparable only to Vigny's Moïse. But unlike this truly supernatural figure, Frenhofer has a flaw:

> "What was obvious to Poussin upon meeting this superhuman being, was a complete image of the artist's nature, that mad nature to which so many powers are entrusted, which abuses them so often, leading cool reason, thoughtful men, and not a few lovers of art, through stony paths where nothing grows. . . . ."[36]

That mad nature, leading to nothingness. Balzac's apparent implication that genius was a function of madness, a typical bit of Romanticism, was seized upon and developed by writers who prided themselves on their scientific objectivity. Balzac himself was oblivious of this implication when he called Joseph Bridau a genius. In this case the term definitely does not connote irrationality or psychological unbalance.

The first step in the special development of the concept is taken by the Goncourts, who give a physiological base to this lack of mental equilibrium. Diagnosing the matter in medical fashion, they decide that geniuses are

> ". . . . men who have sense of infinite delicacy which become exacerbated and exasperated when those agitated, frail and violent natures, those anxious artistic souls, deserving the term of 'troubled geniuses,' react to the pin-pricks of life."[37]

This native predisposition, or *sensitivité malade* as they call it, leads to a local disturbance called the "overstimulation of the painter's artistic organ, his eye." Coriolis, the genius in question, begins to suffer from the fact that "the sense of color, becoming heightened in him, had disturbed, upset, enfevered his vision." His eyes had almost gone mad."[38]

Whatever the merits of this medical discovery, its literary implications are inevitable. Could such a fatal disease have been avoided? Are geniuses always destined to physiological or mental deterioration? The authors have already replied to these questions in making the artist's environment ("the pin-pricks of life") responsible. In Coriolis' case these destructive factors are: lack of moral stamina, an unsatisfactory private life, and an inconsiderate excursion into dangerous ground. The roots of his tragedy are spiritual and ethical as well as physiological. In any event, the conclusions seems to be for the Goncourts that the genius, instead of being particularly strong, is particularly weak.

Zola, who follows the Goncourts in so many ways, adapted their quasi-medical definition of genius to his pseudo-scientific treatment of the principle of heredity. Claude Lantier has all the qualifications of the genius, and he is much more conscious of being one than Coriolis was. This consciousness is of the utmost importance in keeping him steadfast before the most discouraging conditions of poverty, ill-luck and absence of recognition that any painter has ever had to face (at least in fiction). These conditions in themselves would be enough to drive anybody insane. Lantier, however, seems to have the toughness required for survival, until his fatal flaw is uncovered. Like Coriolis, he ventures into experiments with color and light. At this point he begins to lose his self-control. The interest, perhaps intellectual at first, becomes a physical obsession which also deteriorates into a disease or madness of the eye, which affects his mind. (This was not true of Coriolis, whose disability did not attack his reason.) Lantier begins to wonder whether "madness is not the only way out for him,"[39] and suicide his only salvation. Things are not made any easier for him when he overhears whispers of "mad genius," on the part of friends as well as enemies. His friend Sandoz makes the following scientific diagnosis concerning the hereditary significance of Lantier's disease; "He must have suffered in his body, ravaged as it was by the painful lesion of genius; three grams more or less, he used to say, accusing his parents of having built him in such a funny way."[40] These remarks, which form part of the painter's informal funeral oration, lead to further observations that his genius was not "sufficiently clear-cut" for him to have attempted to impose a new formula on the art of his time. We have thus the sub-concept of the "incomplete genius" added to that of the weak genius.

The only literary instance of the equation of genius with mental and physical disequilibrium to be found after *L'Œuvre* is the case of Brignon in *La Ville Lumière*. Nothing is added to the basic concept, the use of which has apparently died out. The 20th Century revises the notion, so far, in two directions. With Romains and Proust, the idea of genius does not connote any kind of weakness. Ortegal is so sure of his genius that its exercise brings a total liberation from ethical or esthetic bonds. He feels himself to be a distinctly superior and stronger being, Nietzschean in his superhuman possibilities, and therefore beyond good and evil, or beauty and ugliness. Ordinary values have no meaning. A genius is a genius by the grace of some mysterious power, and there is no point in arguing with it. It exists for the purpose of expressing itself, and anything and everything which it expresses is of equal validity.

Elstir bears some resemblance to the conventional figure of the genius. He is at first misunderstood and lives "in a state of isolation and wildness that society people called an ill-bred pose, the authorities a rebellious attitude, his neighbors madness, his family selfishness and pride."[41] The narrator who visits him in his retirement finds him affable and decides that his withdrawal from the world is an act of self-dedication to posterity, somewhat mitigated by the pleasures of living alone. After watching the artist at work, examining his canvases and returning several times to converse with him and to test the high caliber of his intellect, the narrator comes to the following conclusions:

> "Artistic genius acts in the manner of those extremely high temperatures which have the power of breaking down combinations of atoms and of regrouping them according to an absolutely contrary order . . . ."[42]

The artist takes his material from life and rearranges it according to his inner vision. He is a creator of universal types, not entirely free from temporal or historical contexts; these, however, are the limitations on the artists; among them, the genius is he who is most capable of the freest interpretations by the fullest use of all the means at his disposal. Thus genius, for Proust, is a symbol of creative force.

* * * * *

One thing French literature grants in common to painting geniuses, whether they be mad, diseased or strong, and that is creative vision, the ability to see Life and to recreate it. Proust and Balzac, separated in time, unite in declaring that the painter's aim is essentially that of the poet. Like him, the painter is Seer, Prophet, Beacon of Mankind, Representative of his epoch, Prometheus Unbound. To Balzac's cry: "Thou art not a vile copyist, thou art a Poet!" we add Hugo's invocation to Albrecht Dürer: "O mon Maitre!" and Baudelaire's glorification of the great painters as *Les Phares*. Not to be outdone by the Romantics, the Naturalists intone the same hymn. To the Goncourts' description of Crescent as one of the Great Hermits, "capable of ecstatic states in his isolation before Nature,"[43] we join Lantier-Zola's incantation:

"Ah, Life, Life! To feel and to render it in its reality, to love it for its own sake, to see in it the only real Beauty, eternal and changeful, to forget the stupid idea that you can ennoble it by castrating it, to understand that ugliness is only the sharp edge of character, and to make things live, to create men, which is the only way to be God!"[44]

The Naturalists then are the ones to make the jump from Poet to God in their idealization of the artist. Lantier's failure must therefore be understood as the result of some divine jealousy. ola's aspiration to divine qualities seems rather tentative when compared with Proust's. Speaking of Elstir's studio, he refers to it as a kind of laboratory:

". . . . . like the laboratory for a new way of creating the world in which the artist, by the very act of painting, draws out of the chaos in which all visible objects move various forms to which he gives definitive meaning; painting thus becomes one of the most fruitful sources of knowledge and of poetic understanding of the universe that man can ever tap, and the painter is akin to God . . ."[45]

This thought is the essence of Proust's ideas on Art, and therefore Elstir, whose personality rather eludes the reader, is perhaps Proust's most significant figure in spite of the relatively short amount of space he occupies in the total work of this writer. He is the most recent expression of the belief that the mission of the artist is that of a teacher and an interpreter of the mystery of life because he creates the only forms through which it may be understood. His ultimate significance to us is that he is a painter, and not a musician or a sculptor or a poet. This fact singularly broadens our basic context, by specifying which Art and which Artist have been elected to carry out the majestic functions announced by the Romantic school more than one hundred years ago.

Romains' ironic treatment of Ortegal seems to be the one discordant note in this concert. Ortegal, insofar as he typifies the artist of our times (and if we except the poet Strigelius, who is highly suggestive of Paul Valéry, Ortegal is the only "artist" in the whole of *Les Hommes de Bonne Volonté* and therefore legitimately to be considered a representative figure) might seem to be a charlatan. And yet he reflects the baffling cross-currents of our century; the world's unrest is discernible in his vague revolutionary leanings. In a time of altering or disappearing values, his cynicism is comprehensible, and he cannot be blamed if expressions like "Ideal Beauty," "artistic integrity" and so forth are meaningless to him. After all, he is engaged in the business of creating forms, and the author is forced to admit that when the painter has overcome all restraining timidities, he enjoys a kind of pleasure that puts him in a superhuman category:

> ". . . . Yes, it is not unpleasant to feel that out of one's self there flows a fountain of mysteries and of truths. The Old Testament Prophets must have felt the same way. If He exists, God, on a larger scale, must feel the same way . . . ."[46]

Romains' painter is hardly comparable with Proust's Elstir since he lacks the latter's elements of universality and is decidedly not a spokesman for the author (except by indirection: Romains' true tastes in painting might be inferred as being in diametric opposition to everything that Picasso-Ortegal stands for). Nor is Ortegal a "man of good will" in the sense in which this term might be applicable to Elstir. Yet he belongs in the great family of artists created by French fiction, whose points of resemblance outnumber their dissimilarities. They all grapple with the same problem, which is to give meaning to the mystery of life. By their very calling they inevitably appear as Romantic figures. The most convinced Naturalistic novelist can hardly retain a matter-of-fact attitude before his painter; he may love him or he may detest him, but he is always excited by him, in spite of himself. It may therefore be said, by way of tentative conclusion, that the portrait of the painter in French fiction is always a conventional one, and that this conventional portrait has remained basically unchanged for more than a hundred years.

The psychological validity of this portrait—or series of related portraits—is therefore open to question. If the novelist cannot be objective as regards the painter, can he ever do him justice, or can he even give us an approximately "true" picture of this type of personality? Without wishing to debate the point as to whether a psychological novelist can always maintain the theoretic objectivity of the scientist, one might state the opinion that "psychological" truth is only one aspect of the truth, by no means superior to "poetic" truth as a means of revealing character and personality or to be preferred to it by the writer. The French novelists who have essayed the character of the painter have treated him poetically, but poetic vision can at times be so accurate as to make mere psychology seem paltry. What truer portrait of the painter is there in all literature than Balzac's Frenhofer, who made Cézanne exclaim, "C'est moi!"? Where are there deeper insights into the nature of the painter than in the portrait of Elstir, made up entirely of intuitive strokes? It all resolves itself into a question of judicious selection; analyses such as the present one are made in the hope of rendering this task easier.

NOTES

1. The influence of *Manette Salomon* on subsequent novels about artists is visible in works by Chesneau, Burty, Duranty, Frantz Jourdain and André Billy. In many ways, *L'Œuvre* follows its pattern closely. Edmond de Goncourt was not unaware of the homage paid to him by his imitators and continuators. *L'Atelier Chantorel* receives a good mark in the *Journal* (Vol. ix, p. 33). There is no mention whatever in it of Zola's novel. According to Vollard (*En Ecoutant Cézanne, Degas, Renoir*, p. 192) Goncourt was furious with Zola for having despoiled him of his "property" by borrowing for his title the first part of the title of the Goncourts' *L'Œuvre de François Boucher*.
2. Cf. especially: Mary W. Scott, *Art and Artists in Balzac's Comédie Humaine.*
3. Théophile Gautier, *Albertus, ou l'Ame et le Péché, 1831.* Some fifty verses are devoted to describing for the "lecteur bourgeois" the studio of Albertus, a gentleman painter. The properties required for this setting are such as to insure its use as "a den, a museum, a boudoir." On the merits of northern exposure in a studio, see Chassagnol's remarks in *Manette Salomon*, pp. 229-230. (All references to this work concern the definitive edition, Paris, 1936). See also Duranty's *L'Atelier.*
4. To which we may join Shaw's anticipatory rejoinder (in *Immaturity*) that artists' wives are always of the middle class.
5. Mauclair, *La Ville Lumière*, pp. 158-159.
6. *Ibid.*, p. 166.
7. Cf. *Lettres de Paul Gauguin à G. D. de Monfreid*; referring to possible biographers, he writes: "Je désire uniquement *le silence*, le *silence*, et encore le *silence.*" (p. 194.)
8. The 1928 edition of *L'Œuvre* contains notes and commentaries by M. Le Blond giving the genesis of this novel. The pregnant passage is found on p. 410: "La question est de savoir ce qui le rend impuissant: lui avant tout, sa physiologie, sa race, la lésion de son œil; mais je voudrais aussi que notre art moderne y fût pour quelque chose, notre fièvre à tout vouloir, notre impatience à secouer les traditions, notre déséquilibrement en un mot."
9. For the Goncourts, marriage is a happiness denied to the artist because he is a kind of "social monster." Whenever they can, they accumulated proofs of a painter's mistake in marrying; cf. the article on Greuze in *l'Art du 18e Siècle*, 2e série. This thesis is also upheld by Octave Feuillet, whose painter marries twice and is unhappy both times.
10. Goncourt, *Journal*, v.ii, entry for May 1, 1864.
11. *Manette Salomon*, p. 437.
12 Balzac, *La Maison du Chat-qui-pelote* (Calmann-Lévy ed., Paris 1884) p. 35.
13. Proust, *A L'Ombre des Jeunes Filles en Fleurs* (1920 edition in 2 volumes) vol. ii, pp. 136-137.
14. Ibid., p. 137.
15. *La Ville Lumière*, p. 13.
16. *Manette Salomon*, pp. 261-266.

17. Balzac, *Le Chef-d'Œuvre Inconnu* (Flammarion edition, Paris, 1927), p. 11.
18. *A L'Ombre des Jeunes Filles*, v. ii, p. 124.
19. *Manette Salomon*, pp. 337-340.
20 Zola, *L'Œuvre* (Fasquelle edition, Paris, 1906), p. 327.
21. The southern accent and violent expressions of Cézanne are played up by Duranty in *Le Peintre Louis Martin*, when he presents that artist under the name of Maillobert; pp. 316-320.
22. Delacroix, *Journal*, v. i, pp. 96-97.
23. Ibid., vol. ii, p. 172.
24. Burty, *Grave Imprudence*, pp. 59-60.
25. Zola, *Mes Haines* (Fasquelle ed., Paris, 1923) pp. 280-282.
26. Cf.: *La Nuit d'Octobre:*

    "L'homme est un apprenti, la douleur est son maître,
    Et nul ne se connait tant qu'il n'a pas souffert."
27. Romains, *Les Hommes de Bonne Volonté*, vol. xiii, pp. 284-285.
28. *Manette Salomon*, p. 185.
29. *Les Hommes de Bonne Volonté*, vol. xii, pp. 162-169, vol. xiii, pp. 267-286.
30. *A L'Ombre des Jeunes Filles en Fleurs*, vol. ii, pp. 124-126.
31. *Manette Salomon*, pp. 273-276.
32. *A L'Ombre des Jeunes Filles*, vol. ii, p. 148.
33. Goncourt, *Journal*, vol. ix, p. 188. This general attitude is echoed by Brignon in *La Ville Lumière*. This painter dies with the conviction that "la peinture est un art fichu" (p. 184).
34. *Manette Salomon*, pp. 467-468.
35. Cf. Ima W. Ebin, "Manet and Zola," *Gazette des Beaux-Arts*, vol. 27:357-378, June, 1945.
36. *Le Chef-d'Œuvre Inconnu*, p. 22.
37. *Manette Salomon*, p. 374.
38. *Ibid.*, pp. 457-458.
39. *L'Œuvre*, p. 331.
40. *Ibid.*, p. 483.
41. *A L'Ombre des Jeunes Filles*, vol. ii, p. 117.
42. *Ibid.*, p. 146.
43. *Manette Salomon*, p. 301.
44. *L'Œuvre*, p. 101.
45. *A L'Ombre des Jeunes Filles*, pp. 122-123.
46. *Les Hommes de Bonne Volonté*, vol. xiii, p. 283.

APPENDIX I

Repertory of the Painters, fictive and real, who Appear in French fiction

a) *Fictive Painters*

Alquier (in Mauclair's *La Ville Lumière*). A talented and successful man who prostitutes his art for the sake of money.

Aurize (in Mauclair's *La Ville Lumière*). An ex-Symbolist who is in process of becoming an Impressionist through his "discovery" of sunlight.

Barbenfeu (in Dorgelès' *Le Château des Brouillards*). A Bohemian with vague anarchistic leanings.

Bargue (in Jourdain's *L'Atelier Chantorel*). A rebel who gives up painting in order to become a dealer in pictures.

Bazoche (in Goncourt's *Manette Salomon*). The most thorough study in French literature of the shiftless but amiable Bohemian.

Bertin (in Maupassant's *Fort Comme la Mort*). A successful society painter involved in a complex love affair.

Bianne (in Banville's *Madame Robert*). A handsome old celebrity who inspires a hopeless love in a young woman.

Bixiou (in many parts of Balzac's *Comédie Humaine*). Trained as a painter, he becomes a famous wit and caricaturist. Patterned on Henri Monnier.

Bongrand (in Zola's *L'Œuvre*). A successful independent artist, presented as genuinely great, though not free from self-doubts. Based, according to the author on "un Manet très chic, ou plutôt un Flaubert."

Joseph Bridau (principally in Balzac's *La Rabouilleuse*, though he also appears elsewhere in the *Comédie Humaine*). An authentic genius traveling the whole path from early trials to fame. Partly based on Delacroix.

Brignon (in Mauclair's *La Ville Lumière*). An unsuccessful genius who dies insane.

Brissot (in Burty's *Grave Imprudence*). A pupil of Delacroix who becomes a "leader of the Impressionist movement." Suggests Monet, with elements of Renoir and Manet. Heavily involved in a love affair.

Pablo Canouris (in Apollinaire's *La Femme Assise*). An albano-hispanic reincarnation of El Greco, also suggestive of Picasso in his blue period.

Chafgrin (in Billy's *Nathalie*). A plein-airist who is in reality an *agent provocateur* of the police.

Chaine (in Zola's *L'Œuvre*). A very mediocre artist, supported by a misguided patron. At bottom, an uneducated rustic.

Chanly (in Chesneau's *La Chimère*). An idealistic commuter between Symbolism and Impressionism. Involved in a love affair.

Chassagnol (in Goncourt's *Manette Salomon*). The classic example of the painter who has given up painting for talking. Patterned on Chenavard.

Chien-Caillou (in Champfleury's *Chien-Caillou*). This competent and promising craftsman dies in abject poverty. Based on Bresdin.

Coriolis (in Goncourt's *Manette Salomon*). A potentially great artist ruined by an unworthy love. His personality is very thoroughly analyzed. Partly based on Tournemine.

Courajod (in Zola's *L'Œuvre*). A landscape painter of admirable qualities. Mostly suggestive of Corot.

Crescent (in Goncourt's *Manette Salomon*). Another landscape painter of equally admirable character. A combination of Diaz, Jaque and Millet.

Delcambre (in Duhamel's *Chronique des Pasquier*, especially *La Nuit de la Saint-Jean*). A pretentious portrait painter.

Delcombe (in Mauclair's *La Ville Lumière*). An artist of integrity, with proletarian sympathies.

Didier (in Billy's *Nathalie*). A would-be painter, who apprentices himself to Balazc's Pierre Grassou.

Lazare Druide (in Léon Bloy's *La Femme Pauvre*). A talented painter of religious subjects. Inspired by the young Rouault.

Dubourdieu (in Balzac's *Les Comédiens Sans le Savoir*). A "symbolic" painter affected by Fourier's theories.

Pierre Durand (in Jourdain's *L'Atelier Chantorel*). An enemy of the bourgeois point of view in art who gives up painting in order to teach in a *lycée*.

Elstir (in Proust's *A L'Ombre des Jeunes Filles en Fleurs*). A second-generation Impressionist, combining many of the conflicting tendencies of his epoch, represented in the plenitude of his fame.

Jacques Fabrice (in Feuillet's *Honneur d'Artiste*). Unfortunate in both of his marriages, once with a lower-class woman possessed of a shrewish character, the next time with an aristocratic young lady in love with his best friend, this painter commits suicide.

Fagerolles (in Zola's *L'Œuvre*). An *arriviste* who sacrifices artistic integrity for success. Based on Guillemet.

Fauvarque (in Adès' *Un Roi Tout Nu*). An unsuccessful but happy painter. A latter-day reincarnation of the Bohemian, but married and idealistic.

Feuillery (in Mauclair's *La Ville Lumière*). An intransigent painter, clearly patterned on Degas.

Nathalie Fontenail (in Billy's *Nathalie*). A pupil of Rosa Bonheur who gives up painting for marriage.

Frenhofer (in Balzac's *Le Chef-d'Œuvre Inconnu*). The prime example of the painter as mad genius.

Garnotelle (in Goncourt's *Manette Salomon*). A mediocrity who wins recognition for irrelevant reasons. Based on Hippolyte Flandrin, unjustly used as the butt of the authors' scorn for the official system.

Grancey (in Goncourt's *Charles Demailly*). A landscape painter who serves as an author's mouthpiece in a novel about writers.

Pierre Grassou (in Balzac's *Pierre Grassou*). A mediocrity who succeeds through stubbornness and a lack of integrity.

Mlle. Hambert (in Duranty's *L'Atelier*). A woman painter courted by two sculptors.

Haricot-Rouge (in Georges-Michel's *Les Montparnos*). A woman painter of talent, involved in a fatal love for Modrulleau. Based on Jeanne Hébuterne.

Kariste (in several sketches by Mirbeau collected in *Des Artistes*). A satirical figment created for critical purposes.

Landry (in Chesneau's *La Chimère*). A successful painter with a typically literary turn of mind.

Langibout (in Goncourt's *Manette Salomon*). The head of the art school frequented by the principal characters in the novel. Patterned on Drolling.

Claude Lantier (in Zola's *L'Œuvre*). A thoroughgoing and relatively sympathetic study of the artist as failure. The basic model is Cézanne.

Laurent (in George Sand's *Elle et Lui*). The hero of the famous love affair whose belief in art for art's sake makes him withdraw into lofty inactivity.

Lavertujeon (in Champfleury's *Les Amis de la Nature*). Possibly a satirical portrait of Courbet, in a rather thin and unconvincing manner.

Léon de Lora (in Balzac's *Un Début dans la Vie* and other parts of *La Comédie Humaine*). A brilliantly successful artist and wit, specializing in landscapes and marines.

Maillobert (in Duranty's *Le Peintre Louis Martin*). A struggling, hot-tempered artist. Vollard's opinion (in his *En Ecoutant Cézanne, etc.*, p. 33) that this character represents Cézanne does not carry conviction.

Monfrey (in Bourget's *La Dame qui a perdu son Peintre*). An elderly, successful artist, involved in a highly romantic affair with a young woman. A variant on the Bohemian who has become successful.

Monsieur Marcel (in Feydeau's *Catherine d'Overmeire*). A self-exiled realist, involved in a very honorable love affair with the heroine, who makes him recant his detached views on art.

Marcel (in Mürger's *Scènes de la Vie de Bohème*). An irresponsible Bohemian.

Marcillon (in Duranty's *L'Atelier*). A sound but undistinguished craftsman.

Louis Martin (in Duranty's *Le Peintre Louis Martin*). A synthesis of various early Impressionists, including Bazille. His brilliant career is cut short by his death in the Franco-Prussian War.

Mazel (in Zola's *L'Œuvre*). A successful academician who patronizes Lantier.

Modrulleau (in Georges-Michel's *Les Montparnos*). This tragic and appealing figure is a combination of Modigliani and Utrillo.

Morsanne (in Mauclair's *La Ville Lumière*). A talented artist whose failure is due to weakness of character.

Munster (in Nodier's *Le Peintre de Saltzbourg*). A painter in the throes of elegiac misery over the death of his sweetheart, the first lady-painter in French literature, *morte-née*, so to speak.

Ortegal (in Romains' *Les Hommes de Bonne Volonté*, vols. xii, xiii, & xx). A satirical portrait of Picasso up to 1920.

Paroli (in Salmon's *La Négresse du Sacré-Cœur*). A cynical painter, presented as a "wealthy, avaricious and quarrelsome Impressionist." Based on Derain.

Pellerin (in Flaubert's *L'Education Sentimentale*). A despairing and cynical artist, not devoid of talent, who ends up as a photographer.

Rochès (in Mauclair's *La Ville Lumière*). An artist of great integrity, whose style suggests Renoir's.

Schaunard (in Mürger's *Scènes de la Vie de Bohème*). A musician-painter.

Schinner (in Balzac's *La Bourse* and other tales). A talented artist, whose career may be followed by interest.

Sentilhe (in Adès' *Un Roi Tout Nu*). An *arriviste*.

Sommervieux (in Balzac's *La Maison du Chat-qui-pelote*). The prototype of the refined Romantic artist.

Sorgue (in Salmon's *La Négresse du Sacré-Cœur*). A sympathetic projection of Picasso in his cubist period.

Thérèse (in George Sand's *Elle et Lui*). The heroine of the famous love affair, characteristically presented as a hard-working artist.

Thomas (in Champfleury's Les Aventures de *Mlle. Mariette*). Suggestive of Couture.

Turrio (in Banville's *La Pose*). A famous artist who will not let love interfere with his work.

Pomponio Vecellio (in Musset's *Le Fils du Titien*). A talented son of the great Titian who accounts art well lost for love.

Vénius (in Erckmann-Chatrian's *L'Esquisse Mystérieuse*). Unjustly accused of a crime, his skill as a draftsman saves his life.

Weuille (in Mauclair's *La Ville Lumière*). A rosicrucian mystic and painter of allegories, whose style recalls those of Gustave Moreau and Odilon Redon.

b) *Real Painters*

Boldini Briefly but savagely sketched under the name of Luzzoli in Mauclair's *La Ville Lumière.*

Bonvin Makes a brief appearance in Billy's *Nathalie.*

Bresdin The hero of Champfleury's *Chien-Caillou.* His work is described in detail in Huysmans' *A Rebours.*

Corot Most probably the model for Courajod in Zola's *L'Œuvre.*

Courbet Appears in Champfleury's *Les Amants de la Nature,* Duranty's *Le Peintre Louis Martin* and Billy's *Nathalie.*

Degas Appears as Feuillary in Mauclair's *Le Ville Lumière.*

Derain Satirized as Paroli in Salmon's *La Négresse du Sacré-Cœur.*

Diaz The most important element in the figure of Crescent in Goncourt's *Manette Salomon.*

Gérard, Girodet, Gros These three famous painters make frequent but brief appearances in Balzac's *Comédie Humaine,* usually as teachers and friends of such characters as Bridau, Sommervieux, Schinner and others.

Kisling Appears in Georges-Michel's *Les Montparnos.*

J.-P. Laurens Under the name of Antonio, subject of a biographical novel by F. Fabre, *Le Roman d'un Peintre.*

Manet Appears in person in Duranty's *Le Peintre Louis Martin* and as Bongrand in Zola's *L'Œuvre.*

Monnier Appears as Bixiou in *La Comédie Humaine.*

Picasso Appears under his own name in *Les Montparnos,* as Canouris in *La Femme Assise,* as Sorgue in *La Négresse du Sacré-Cœur,* and as Ortegal in *Les Hommes de Bonne Volonté.*

Pourbus Appears in Balzac's *Le Chef-d'Œuvre Inconnu.*

Poussin Appears in the same work as above.

Guido Reni Appears in Marmontel's *Les Souvenirs du Coin du Feu.*

Rouault Appears as Lazare Druide in Bloy's *La Femme Pauvre.*

Théodore Rousseau Appears under his own name and in a characteristically generous light in Billy's *Nathalie.*

Soutine Appears in *Les Montparnos.*

Horace Vernet Appears in *La Maison du Chat-qui-pelote.*

APPENDIX II

A Selective Gallery of Pictures Painted by Artists in French Fiction

This *catalogue raisonné,* giving an account of the circumstances under which these pictures were painted, their probable date, and titles which are sometimes arbitrarily assigned, may be value in determining an author's understanding of the painter's main function.

Portrait of Beatrice Donato, by Pomponio Vecellio, end of the 16th century. This shows the artist's mistress against a background which contains a rock. On this rock is inscribed the sonnet in which the painter indicates his renunciation of Art for Love:

> "Béatrix Donato fut le doux nom de celle
> Dont la forme terrestre eut ce divin contour.
> Dans sa blanche poitrine était un cœur fidèle,
> Et dans son corps sans tache un esprit sans détour.
>
> Le fils du Titien, pour la rendre immortelle,
> Fit ce portrait, témoin d'un mutuel amour;
> Puis il cessa de peindre à compter de ce jour,
> Ne voulant de sa main illustrer d'autre qu'elle.
>
> Passant, qui que tu sois, si ton cœur sait aimer,
> Regarde ma maitresse avant de me blâmer,
> Et dis si, par hasard, la tienne est aussi belle.
>
> Vois donc combien c'est peu que la gloire ici-bas,
> Puisque, tout beau qu'il est, ce portrait ne vaut pas
> (Crois-m'en sur ma parole) un baiser du modèle."

La Belle Noiseuse, by Frenhofer, about 1612. Known as the "Unknown Masterpiece;" at the time when it was seen by Pourbus and Poussin it had been progressively painted out until a part of a foot remained visible. Destroyed by the artist just before his death.

Portrait of Augustine Guillaume, by Théodore de Sommervieux, about 1807. Painted mostly from memory by the artist in love with a young woman he had not yet met. Received a prize at the 1807 Salon.

Interior, by the same artist, same year. Done in the Dutch style (that is, as realistic *genre* picture), it also won a prize at the 1807 Salon and created a "revolution in painting."

Young Courtesan brought by an Old Woman to a Venetian Senator, by Joseph Bridau. Exhibited at the 1823 Salon and mistaken by Baron Gros for a work by Titian.

The Crossing of the Red Sea, by Marcel, painted and repainted between 1845 and 1850. Consistently turned down at the Salon, where it is sometimes presented as the "Crossing of the Beresina," it finally becomes "The Port of Marseilles" and is used as a shop sign.

The Humanitarian Christ, by Anatole Bazoche, started in 1846. It is a vast allegorical composition containing all of the artist's Utopian aspirations. It ends up as a backdrop for a pantomime show.

Turkish Women's Bath, by Coriolis, about 1852. The first important picture by this artist for which Manette Salomon poses. The central figures are reminiscent of those in Bazille's "Le Bain Turc," now in the Musée Fabre in Montpellier.

The Medical Examination and *Church Wedding*, both painted by Coriolis for the 1855 Exposition. An evident concession to the modern movement towards realism led by Courbet. Both works were indifferently received by the public. Several years later, the first one was sold for a large sum, at no profit to the artist, who ceased to exhibit after this period.

Gylippe, by Gaston de Chanly, about 1860. Done in the Pre-Raphaelite manner, this portrait of a medieval knight is to be interpreted as a symbol of the painter's secret longings.

Portrait of Madame de x. . . ., by the former, about 1863. This portrait of the artist's mistress symbolizes Modern Woman.

Plein Air, by Claude Lantier, painted in 1863 and exhibited at the *Salon des Refusés*. Highly reminiscent of Manet's "Déjeuner à la Campagne."

The Dead Child, by the former, about 1867. The son of the artist on his deathbed. The nature of the subject and its realistic treatment brought highly unfavorable comments to this painting, one of the very few by this artist ever accepted by a Salon.

Paris from the Seine, by the former, worked on between 1865 and 1867. A synthesis of allegory and realism, this painting, conceived entirely by Zola, is meant to be a failure from the start. The enormous canvas was destroyed by Sandoz after Lantier's suicide.

From My Window, by Louis Martin, about 1868. This picture, painted with a plunging perspective, shows women and children against a background of trees and flowers. In the early Impressionist manner, it exudes "an immense sensation of happiness."

The Chimera, by Jean Landry, about 1871. Painted as a memorial to the painter Chanly, this work strongly suggests Gustave Moreau and Redon.

Modern War, by Pierre Durand, about 1872. A realistic rendering of a field of battle by a talented but discouraged artist.

View of the Seine, by Brissot, about 1874. An Impressionistic work, combining the manners of Manet, Monet and Renoir. The first authentic masterpiece by this artist and a landmark in the development of the school's technique.

Le Port de Carquethuit, by Elstir, about 1890. A poetic interpretation of Manet's "Port de Bordeaux."

Algebraic Portrait of a Woman, by Ortegal, about 1914. A more or less abstract puzzle, not composed but dictated by whim. The author reveals here his lack of comprehension of the artist he is satirizing.

DESCRIPTIVE BIBLIOGRAPHY

Novels and stories in which Painters appear as Characters

Except when noted, all citations refer to the first edition or the edition for which the date of publication is given below. All translations are by the author. Significant works are marked by an asterisk.

1803 Charles Nodier: *Le Peintre de Saltzbourg.* A short story in which the painter makes his initial bow into French literature. Told in the first person, it deals with the Wertherian sufferings of a young artist bemoaning the death of his beloved, also a painter.

1818 Marmontel: *Les Souvenirs du Coin du Feu.* A portmanteau set of tales, of which one introduces the figure of Guido Reni as the prototype of the Romantic seeker after ideal beauty.

1830 *Balzac: *La Maison du Chat-qui-pelote.* The story of a sensitive and gifted artist whose marriage fails because his wife cannot appreciate the "finer things of life."

1831 *Balzac: *Le Chef-d'Œuvre Inconnu.* This greatest of all tales on the subject of the painter is a sardonic comment on the futility of perfectionism as well as a tribute to the artist's overwhelming devotion to his esthetic credo.

1832 Balzac: *La Bourse.* A portrait of the starving artist in love.

1838 *Musset: *Le Fils du Titien.* A very plausible tale of a supposed son of Titian, capable of continuing the paternal tradition but anxious to renounce art for love.

1839 *Balzac: *Pierre Grassou.* A satire on an untalented man who stumbles into painting and who is able to achieve success largely through lack of scruples.

1839 Balzac: *La Rabouilleuse.* This long novel is more concerned with the affairs of the brother of the painter Joseph Bridau than with his own, but there is a valuable picture of the life of artists under the First Empire and the Restauration. Based in part on the respective lives of the brothers Charles and Eugène Delacroix.

Other short stories by Balzac, including *Un Début dans la Vie, Les Comédiens sans le Savoir,* and longer works in *La Comédie Humaine,* have painters among their characters. Fuller details will be found in the various studies on Balzac's treatment of artists.

1845 Théophile Gautier: *Feuillets de l'Album d'un Rapin.* A thin jocular tale of a dauber who has his hour of modernistic revolt but falls back into an acceptably pallid mold.

1847 *Champfleury: *Chien-Caillou.* A short story realistically depicting the desperate straits to which true artists may be reduced.

1851 Mürger: *Scènes de la Vie de Bohème.* The classic novel popularizing the myth of the gay, irresponsible artist.

1856 Champfleury: *Les Aventures de Mlle. Mariette.* A short story about a model's life on the periphery of the art world.

1859 George Sand: *Elle et Lui.* Both the protagonists in this version of a famous love affair are turned into painters, but there is more about love than about art here.

1860 Champfleury: *Les Amis de la Nature.* A satire on Courbet and the Realists by a former supporter.

1860 Ernest Feydeau: *Catherine d'Overmeire.* A novel dealing with the sentimental misfortunes of a young woman whose life is finally redeemed by the love of a worthy painter.

1860 Erckmann-Chatrian: *L'Esquisse Mystérieuse* (in their *Contes Fantastiques*). A Hoffmannesque tale in which a painter's dream, translated into a sketch, helps to solve a murder.

1866 Gautier: *Le Berger.* A short story describing the way in which an untutored peasant becomes a successful "primitive" under the influence of love.

1866 *Edmond & Jules de Goncourt: *Manette Salomon.* The classic novel of the painter's life and the most important work of its kind in French literature. A vigorous statement of the art-for-art's sake point of view, an attack on the academic and romantic traditions, a history of the development of landscape painting in France, are some of the many elements which fill this book. The authors also analyze and dissect a variety of painters.

1869 Flaubert: *L'Education Sentimentale.* The hero, who starts out by wanting to be a painter, hovers on the fringes of the Parisian art world.

1873 Alphonse Daudet: *Les Femmes D'Artistes.* A collection of short stories affording an oblique glimpse into the lives of painters, among other artists.

1878 Fabre: *Le Roman d'un Peintre.* A biographical novel, highly sentimentalized, of the painter J.-P. Laurens.

1879 Chesneau: *La Chimère.* This novel throws some light on a forgotten phase in the history of French painting, a species of Pre-Raphaelitism, in which Parnassian symbolism is allied with standard Impressionism.

1880 *Burty: *Grave Imprudence.* A novel dealing with the artistic growth of a leading Impressionist by one of the early sympathetic critics of the movement.

1881 *Duranty: *Le Pays des Arts.* Four short stories about art, of which two, "Le Peintre Louis Martin" and "L'Atelier" are especially valuable as a record of the early days of Impressionism.

1881-1887 Théodore de Banville. His collected short stories, originally appearing in the periodical press, contain several dealing with painters. The best ones are "Madame Robert" and "La Pose."

1885 *Zola: *L'Œuvre.* The most controversial novel on the subject of the painter. *The author's reliability as art critic and connoisseur is in question; his lack of objectivity, his misunderstanding of modern tendencies in painting, his misuse of the personality of Cézanne as a model for his hero, and other faults have long been targets for abuse. The novel is nevertheless very moving in its re-creation of the heroic days of 1863-1866, when the writer was fighting for the right of new artists to be heard.

1889 Maupassant: *Fort Comme la Mort.* A novel describing the sentimental involvements of a successful academic painter.

1890 Octave Feuillet: *Honneur d'Artiste.* This novel stresses the marital misfortunes of an honorable artist. It will be noted that like

Maupassant's hero in the preceding novel, Feuillet's artist belongs to the academic tradition.

1893 *Frantz Jourdain: *L'Atelier Chantorel.* This novel, though mostly concerned with the problems of the architect between 1867 and 1890, is valuable for the insights it gives into the painter's situation within those dates.

1897 Léon Bloy: *La Femme Pauvre.* Some aspects of modern religious painting are treated in this famous polemical novel.

1903 *Camille Mauclair: *La Ville Lumière.* Paris as the art center of the world in the last decade of the 19th century. Dozens of painters, under their own name or under transparent disguises, populate the pages of this novel, whose merit as a document is greater than its psychological value.

1907 Paul Bourget: *La Dame qui a perdu son Peintre.* An ironic *novella* satirizing connoisseurship, scientific art critics and the gentle art of forgery.

1918 *Proust: *A L'Ombre des Jeunes Filles en Fleurs.* A small but significant section of this part of *A La Recherche du Temps Perdu* is devoted to the author's projection of a painter who synthesizes the conflicting tendencies of Impressionism and Post-Impressionism and who bespeaks the author's philosophy of art.

1920 André Salmon: *La Négresse du Sacré-Cœur.* A novel of the artist's life in Montmartre in the early days of Cubism.

1920 Apollinaire: *La Femme Assise.* Chapter II of this curious novel on Mormonism deals with early Cubists.

1922 Adès: *Un Roi Tout Nu.* An unfinished novel, published posthumously, contrasting a bad but successful painter with a happy failure.

1929 *Michel Georges-Michel: *Les Montparnos.* A novel of the last Bohemia after the first World War.

1932 Dorgelès: *Le Château des Brouillards.* A novel of Bohemian life in Montmartre before the first World War; the role of the painter is very secondary.

1936-1941 *Romains: *Les Hommes de Bonne Volonté.* Vols xii. xiii and xx deal in part with the representative figure of a painter who symbolizes the artistic anarchy of the period before 1914.

1938 Billy: *Nathalie.* A historical novel dealing with the innocent involvement of several painters in a plot to assassinate Napoleon III. Interesting for its attempt to recreate the atmosphere of Barbizon.

Duhamel's *Chronique des Pasquier* (1935-1939) contains some discussions of modern painting. *La Route D'Emeraude* (Paris, 1924), by the Belgian author Eugène Demolder, is a historical novel of the times of Rembrandt. Also to be noted are the stories about painters by the Swiss author Edouard Rod: *Les Allemands à Paris* (1880) and *La Femme d'Henri Vannaux* (1884).

ADDITIONAL BIBLIOGRAPHY

Baudelaire, C. *L'Art Romantique*; édition définitive, Paris, Calmann-Lévy, 1919.

Chernowitz, M. E. *Proust and Painting*; International University Press, New York, 1945.

Delacroix, E. *Journal*; 3 vols., Plon, Paris, 1932.

Eben, I. N. "Manet and Zola," *Gazette des Beaux-Arts*, v. 27:357-378, New York, June 1945.

Fosca, F. "Les Artistes dans les romans de Balzac," *Revue critique des idées et des livres*, v. 35:133-152, Paris, 1922.

Fosca, F. *E. et J. de Goncourt*; Albin Michel, Paris, 1941.

Gauguin, P. *Lettres à G. D. de Monfreid*; Crès, Paris, 1918.

Goncourt, E. et J. *Charles Demailly*; édit. déf., Flammarion-Fasquelle, Paris, 1926.

Goncourt, E. et J. *Journal*, édit. déf., Flammarion-Fasquelle, Paris, 1935-1936.

Rewald, J. *Cézanne*; Albin Michel, Paris, 1939.

Rewald, J. *The History of Impressionism*; The Museum of Modern Art, New York, 1946.

Scott, E. W. *Art and Artists in Balzac's Comédie Humaine*; Chicago University Press, Chicago, 1937.

Valéry, P. *Degas, Danse, Dessin*; Gallimard, Paris, 1938.

Venturi, L. *Les Archives de l'Impressionisme*, 2 vols. Durand-Ruel, Paris-New York, 1939.

Vollard, A. *En Ecoutant Cézanne, Degas, Renoir*; Grasset, Paris, 1938.

Zola, E. *Mes Haines*; Fasquelle, Paris, 1923.

www.ingramcontent.com/pod-product-compliance
Lightning Source LLC
LaVergne TN
LVHW050945080826
845145LV00004B/1413
9780807890158